W9-CQA-053

MEMORIALS OF THE FAITHFUL

‘Abdu’l-Bahá

Memorials of the Faithful

by

'ABDU'L-BAHÁ

Translated from the original Persian text and annotated by Marzieh Gail

BAHÁ'Í PUBLISHING TRUST
WILMETTE, ILLINOIS

Second Printing 1975

Standard Book Number: 0-87743-041-1
Library of Congress Catalog Card Number: 77–157797

Printed in the United States of America

This translation is dedicated to
Shoghi Effendi
Guardian of the Bahá'í Faith

Love alters not with his brief hours

ACKNOWLEDGEMENTS

For consultation on certain Persian and Arabic terms, grateful acknowledgement is made to Ali-Kuli Khan, Nabílu'd-Dawlih, Mrs. Bahia Gulick, and Allah K.Kalántar, as well as to Dr. Amín Banání who helpfully compared the Persian original with the present text.

THE TRANSLATOR

CONTENTS

CONTENTS

Nota bene. There is no standard English Qur'án text. The original and several translations were used by the translator, with the preference given to Rodwell. Súrih and verse numbers are as in Rodwell.

PROEM

This is a book about people who were trying to get into prison rather than to escape from it, because they were prisoners of a great love. Their love was for Bahá'u'lláh, Whom the nineteenth century world bound with chains and tried to silence by shutting Him, ultimately, in the Crusaders' stronghold at 'Akká. Like the eye of the storm, He is the center of these accounts, but hardly appears in them—remaining, as the Guardian has described Him, "transcendental in His majesty, serene, awe-inspiring, unapproachably glorious."

The reader will probably find himself in these pages, whether he is the jeweler from Baghdád, one of the dishwashers, or the professor who could not endure the arrogance of his compeers. Mystic, feminist, cleric, artisan, merchant prince are here. Even modern Western youth will be found here, for example in the chapter on dervishes. For this is more than the brief annals of early Bahá'í disciples; it is, somehow, a book of prototypes; and it is a kind of testament of values endorsed and willed to us by the Bahá'í Exemplar, values now derided, but—if the planet is to be made safe for humanity—indispensable. These are short and simple accounts, but they constitute a manual of how to live, and how to die.

The task of putting these biographies into English was given me by the Guardian many years ago, when I was on a pilgrimage to the Bahá'í world center in Haifa. Shortly afterward the Guardian sent me, to Ṭihrán, the text from which this translation was made. According to its Persian title page, this was the first Bahá'í book to be printed in Haifa under the Guardianship. A Persian introduction states that 'Abdu'l-Bahá wrote the book in 1915, and granted permission to M. A. Kahrubá'í to have it published. The text, which is dated 1924, bears the seal of the Haifa Bahá'í Assembly. A second title page, in English, describes the work as "An account, from the pen of 'Abdu'l-Bahá, of the lives of some of the early Bahá'í believers who passed away during His lifetime," although the work was actually recorded from His utterances.

Here, then, almost half a century after His passing, is a new book given to the world by 'Abdu'l-Bahá.

We wonder how many of us, at the close of unbelievably painful and arduous years, would devote the waning time not to our own memories but to the lives of some seventy companions, many of them long dead, to save them from oblivion. 'Abdu'l-Bahá was present at many of these scenes, yet time after time He effaces Himself to focus on some companion, often on one so humble that the passing years would surely have refused him a history. And if, to the cynical, these believers seem better than ordinary men, we should remember that the presence of the Manifestation made them so, and that they are being looked at through the eyes of the Master—Who said that the imperfect eye beholds imperfections, and that it is easier to please God than to please people.

Thus the book is still another token of 'Abdu'l-Bahá's partiality for the human race. The love He personified was not blind but observant, not impersonal but warm and tender; it was a continual attitude of unobtrusive care. Such love, from such a Being, does not end with one lifespan. He left the world half a century ago, and most of those who longed for Him so much that the hostile said they were not Bahá'ís, but 'Abdu'l-Bahá'ís, are now vanished from our sight. But still, His love is here, for new millions to find.

THE TRANSLATOR

Keene, New Hampshire, December 1969

MEMORIALS OF THE FAITHFUL

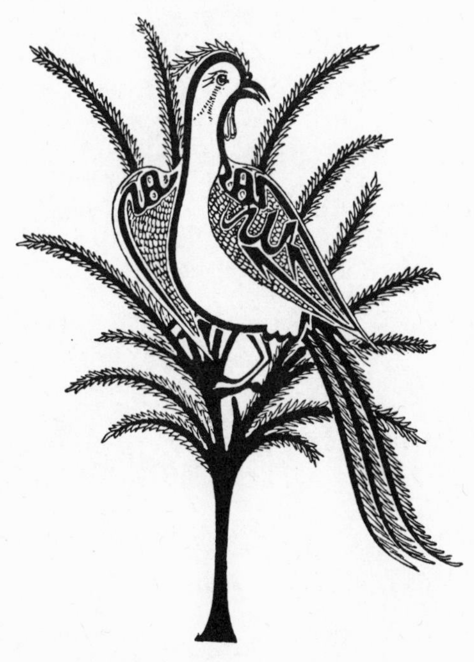

Nabíl-i-Akbar

There was, in the city of Najaf, among the disciples of the widely known mujtahid, Shaykh Murtaḍá, a man without likeness or peer. His name was Áqá Muḥammad-i-Qá'iní, and later on he would receive, from the Manifestation, the title of Nabíl-i-Akbar.[1] This eminent soul became the leading member of the mujtahid's company of disciples. Singled out from among them all, he alone was given the rank of mujtahid—for the late Shaykh Murtaḍá was never wont to confer this degree.

He excelled not only in theology but in other branches of knowledge, such as the humanities, the philosophy of the Illuminati, the teachings of the mystics and of the Shaykhí School. He was a universal man, in himself alone a convincing proof. When his eyes were opened to the light of Divine guidance, and he breathed in the fragrances of Heaven, he became a flame of God. Then his heart leapt within him, and in an ecstasy of joy and love, he roared out like leviathan in the deep.

With praises showered upon him, he received his new rank from the mujtahid. He then left Najaf and came to Baghdád, and here he was honored with meeting Bahá'u'lláh. Here he beheld the light that blazed on Sinai in the Holy Tree. Soon he was in such a state that he could rest neither day nor night.

[1] For the author of *The Dawn-Breakers,* see Nabíl-i-Zarandí.

One day, on the floor of the outer apartments reserved for the men, the honored Nabíl was reverently kneeling in the presence of Bahá'u'lláh. At that moment Ḥájí Mírzá Ḥasan-'Amú, a trusted associate of the mujtahids of Karbilá, came in with Zaynu'l-'Ábidín Khán, the Fakhru'd-Dawlih. Observing how humbly and deferentially Nabíl was kneeling there, the Ḥají was astonished.

"Sir," he murmured, "what are you doing in this place?"

Nabíl answered, "I came here for the same reason you did."

The two visitors could not recover from their surprise, for it was widely known that this personage was unique among mujtahids and was the most favored disciple of the renowned Shaykh Murtaḍá.

Later, Nabíl-i-Akbar left for Persia and went on to Khurásán. The Amír of Qá'in—Mír 'Alam Khán—showed him every courtesy at first, and greatly valued his company. So marked was this that people felt the Amír was captivated by him, and indeed he was spellbound at the scholar's eloquence, knowledge, and accomplishments. One can judge, from this, what honors were accorded to Nabíl by the rest, for "men follow the faith of their kings."

Nabíl spent some time thus esteemed and in high favor, but the love he had for God was past all concealing. It burst from his heart, flamed out and consumed its coverings.

A thousand ways I tried
My love to hide—
But how could I, upon that blazing pyre
Not catch fire!

He brought light to the Qá'in area and converted a great number of people. And when he had become known far and wide by this new name, the clergy, envious and malevolent, arose, and informed against him, sending their calumnies on to Ṭihrán, so that Náṣiri'd-Dín S͟háh rose up in wrath. Terrified of the S͟háh, the Amír attacked Nabíl with all his might. Soon the whole city was in an uproar, and the populace, lashed to fury, turned upon him.

That enraptured lover of God never gave way, but withstood them all. At last, however, they drove him out—drove out that man who saw what they did not—and he went up to Ṭihrán, where he was a fugitive, and homeless.

Here, his enemies struck at him again. He was pursued by the watchmen; guards looked everywhere for him, asking after him in every street and alley, hunting him down to catch and torture him. Hiding, he would pass by them like the sigh of the oppressed, and rise to the hills; or again, like the tears of the wronged, he would slip down into the valleys. He could no longer wear the turban denoting his rank; he disguised himself, putting on a layman's hat, so that they would fail to recognize him and would let him be.

In secret, with all his powers he kept on spreading the Faith and setting forth its proofs, and was a guiding lamp to many souls. He was exposed to danger at all times, always vigilant and on his guard. The Government never gave up its search for him, nor did the people cease from discussing his case.

He left, then, for Buk͟hárá and 'Is͟hqábád, continuously teaching the Faith in those regions. Like a candle, he was using up his life; but in spite of his sufferings he was never dispirited, rather his joy and ardor increased with every passing day. He was eloquent of speech; he was a skilled physician, a remedy for every ill, a balm to every sore. He would guide the Illuminati by their own philosophical principles, and with the mystics he would prove the Divine Advent in terms of "inspiration" and the "celestial vision." He would convince the Shaykhí leaders by quoting the very words of their late Founders, Shaykh Aḥmad and Siyyid Káẓim, and would convert Islamic theologians with texts from the Qur'án and traditions from the Imáms, who guide mankind aright. Thus he was an instant medicine to the ailing, and a rich bestowal to the poor.

He became penniless in Bukhárá and a prey to many troubles, until at the last, far from his homeland, he died, hastening away to the Kingdom where no poverty exists.

Nabíl-i-Akbar was the author of a masterly essay demonstrating the truth of the Cause, but the friends do not have it in hand at the present time. I hope that it will come to light, and will serve as an admonition to the learned. It is true that in this swiftly passing world he was the target of countless woes; and yet, all those generations of powerful clerics, those shaykhs like Murtaḍá and Mírzá Ḥabíbu'lláh and Áyatu'lláh-i-Khurásání and Mullá Asadu'lláh-i-Mázandarání—all of them will disappear without a trace. They will leave no name behind them, no sign, no fruit. No word will be passed down from any of them; no man will tell of them again. But because he stood steadfast in this holy Faith, because he guided souls and served this Cause and spread its fame, that star, Nabíl, will shine forever from the horizon of abiding light.

It is clear that whatever glory is gained outside the Cause of God turns to abasement at the end; and ease and comfort not met with on the path of God are finally but care and sorrow; and all such wealth is penury, and nothing more.

A sign of guidance, he was, an emblem of the fear of God. For this Faith, he laid down his life, and in dying, triumphed. He passed by the world and its rewards; he closed his eyes to rank and wealth; he loosed himself from all such chains and fetters, and put every worldly thought aside. Of wide learning, at once a mujtahid, a philosopher, a mystic, and gifted with intuitive sight, he was also an accomplished man of letters and an orator without a peer. He had a great and universal mind.

Praise be to God, at the end he was made the recipient of heavenly grace. Upon him be the glory of God, the All-Glorious. May God shed the brightness of the Abhá Kingdom upon his resting-place. May God welcome him into the Paradise of reunion, and shelter him forever in the realm of the righteous, submerged in an ocean of lights.

Ismu'lláhu'l-Aṣdaq

Among the Hands of the Cause of God who have departed this life and ascended to the Supreme Horizon was Jináb-i-Ismu'lláhu'l-Aṣdaq. Another was Jináb-i-Nabíl-i-Akbar. Still others were Jináb-i-Mullá 'Alí-Akbar and Jináb-i-Shaykh Muḥammad-Riḍáy-i-Yazdí. Again, among others, was the revered martyr, Áqá Mírzá Varqá.

Ismu'lláhu'l-Aṣdaq was truly a servant of the Lord from the beginning of life till his last breath. When young, he joined the circle of the late Siyyid Káẓim and became one of his disciples. He was known in Persia for his purity of life, winning fame as Mullá Ṣádiq the saintly. He was a blessed individual, a man accomplished, learned, and much honored. The people of Khurásán were strongly attached to him, for he was a great scholar and among the most renowned of matchless and unique divines. As a teacher of the Faith, he spoke with such eloquence, such extraordinary power, that his hearers were won over with great ease.

After he had come to Baghdád and attained the presence of Bahá'u'lláh, he was seated one day in the courtyard of the men's apartments, by the little garden. I was in one of the rooms just above, that gave onto the courtyard. At that moment a Persian prince, a grandson of Fath-'Alí Sháh, arrived at the house. The prince said to him, "Who are you?" Ismu'lláh answered, "I am a servant of this Threshhold. I am one of the keepers of this door." And as I listened from above, he began to teach the Faith. The prince at first objected violently; and yet, in a quarter of an hour, gently and benignly, Jináb-i-Ismu'lláh had quieted him down. After the prince had so sharply denied what was said, and his face had so clearly reflected his fury, now his wrath was changed to smiles and he expressed the greatest satisfaction at having encountered Ismu'lláh and heard what he had to say.

He always taught cheerfully and with gaiety, and would respond gently and with good humor, no matter how much passionate anger might be turned against him by the one with whom he spoke. His way of teaching was excellent. He was truly Ismu'lláh, the Name of God, not for his fame but because he was a chosen soul.

Ismu'lláh had memorized a great number of Islámic traditions and had mastered the teachings of Shaykh Aḥmad and Siyyid Káẓim. He became a believer in Shíráz, in the early days of the Faith, and was soon widely known as such. And because he began to teach openly and boldly, they hung a halter on him and led him about the streets and bázárs of the city. Even in that condition, composed and smiling, he kept on speaking to the people. He did not yield; he was not silenced. When they freed him he left Shíráz and went to Khurásán, and there, too, began to spread the Faith, following which he traveled on, in the company of Bábu'l-Báb, to Fort Ṭabarsí. Here he endured intense sufferings as a member of that band of sacrificial victims. They took him prisoner at the Fort and delivered him over to the chiefs of Mázindarán, to lead him about and finally kill him in a certain district of that province. When, bound with chains, Ismu'lláh was brought to the appointed place, God put it into one man's heart to free him from prison in the middle of the night and guide him to a place where he was safe. Throughout all these agonizing trials he remained staunch in his faith.

Think, for example, how the enemy had completely hemmed in the Fort, and were endlessly pouring in cannon balls from their siege guns. The believers, among them Ismu'lláh, went eighteen days without food. They lived on the leather of their shoes. This too was soon consumed, and they had nothing left but water. They drank a mouthful every morning, and lay famished and exhausted in their Fort. When attacked, however, they would instantly spring to their feet, and manifest in the face of the enemy a magnificent courage and astonishing resistance, and drive the army back from their walls. The hunger lasted eighteen days. It was a terrible ordeal. To begin with, they were far from home, surrounded and cut off by the foe; again, they were starving; and then there were the army's sudden onslaughts and the bombshells raining down and bursting in the heart of the Fort. Under such circumstances to maintain an unwavering faith and patience is extremely difficult, and to endure such dire afflictions a rare phenomenon.[1]

Ismu'lláh did not slacken under fire. Once freed, he taught more widely than ever. He spent every waking breath in calling the people to the Kingdom of God. In

[1] Cf. Nabíl, *The Dawn-Breakers,* p. 395, note 1.

'Iráq, he attained the presence of Bahá'u'lláh, and again in the Most Great Prison, receiving from Him grace and favor.

He was like a surging sea, a falcon that soared high. His visage shone, his tongue was eloquent, his strength and steadfastness astounding. When he opened his lips to teach, the proofs would stream out; when he chanted or prayed, his eyes shed tears like a spring cloud. His face was luminous, his life spiritual, his knowledge both acquired and innate; and celestial was his ardor, his detachment from the world, his righteousness, his piety and fear of God.

Ismu'lláh's tomb is in Hamadán. Many a Tablet was revealed for him by the Supreme Pen of Bahá'u'lláh, including a special Visitation Tablet after his passing. He was a great personage, perfect in all things.

Such blessed beings have now left this world. Thank God, they did not linger on, to witness the agonies that followed the ascension of Bahá'u'lláh—the intense afflictions; for firmly rooted mountains will shake and tremble at these, and the high-towering hills bow down.

He was truly Ismu'lláh, the Name of God. Fortunate is the one who circumambulates that tomb, who blesses himself with the dust of that grave. Upon him be salutations and praise in the Abhá Realm.

Mullá 'Alí-Akbar

Yet another Hand of the Cause was the revered Mullá 'Alí-Akbar, upon him be the glory of God, the All-Glorious. Early in life, this illustrious man attended institutions of higher learning and labored diligently, by day and night, until he became thoroughly conversant with the learning of the day, with secular studies, philosophy, and religious jurisprudence. He frequented the gatherings of philosophers, mystics, and S͟hayk͟hís, thoughtfully traversing those areas of knowledge, intuitive wisdom, and illumination; but he thirsted after the wellspring of truth, and hungered for the bread that comes down from Heaven. No matter how he strove to perfect himself in those regions of the mind, he was never satisfied; he never reached the goal of his desires; his lips stayed parched; he was confused, perplexed, and felt that he had wandered from his path. The reason was that in all those circles he had found no passion; no joy, no ecstasy; no faintest scent of love. And as he went deeper into the core of those manifold beliefs, he discovered that from the day of the Prophet Muḥammad's advent until our own times, innumerable sects have arisen: creeds differing among themselves; disparate opinions, divergent goals, uncounted roads and ways. And he found each one, under some plea or other, claiming to reveal spiritual truth; each one believing that it alone followed the true path—this although the Muḥammedic sea could rise in one great tide, and carry all those sects away to the ocean floor. "No cry shalt thou hear from them, nor a whisper even." [1]

Whoso ponders the lessons of history will learn that this sea has lifted up innumerable waves, yet in the end each has dissolved and vanished, like a shadow drifting by. The waves have perished, but the sea lives on. This is why 'Alí Qabl-i-Akbar could never quench his thirst, till the day when he stood on the shore of Truth and cried:

Here is a sea with treasure to the brim;
Its waves toss pearls under the great wind's thong.
Throw off your robe and plunge, nor try to swim,
Pride not yourself on swimming—dive headlong.

Like a fountain, his heart welled and jetted forth; meaning and truth, like soft-flowing crystal waters, began to stream from his lips. At first, with humility, with spiritual poverty, he garnered the new light, and only then he proceeded to shed it abroad. For how well has it been said,

Shall he the gift of life to others bear
Who of life's gift has never had a share?

A teacher must proceed in this way: he must first teach himself, and then others. If he himself still walks the path of carnal appetites and lusts, how can he guide another to the "evident signs" [2] of God?

This honored man was successful in converting a multitude. For the sake of God he cast all caution aside, as he hastened along the ways of love. He became as one fren-

[1] Cf. Qur'án 19:98

[2] Qur'án 3:91

zied, as a vagrant and one known to be mad. Because of his new Faith, he was mocked at in Ṭihrán by high and low. When he walked through the streets and bázárs, the people pointed their fingers at him, calling him a Bahá'í. Whenever trouble broke out, he was the one to be arrested first. He was always ready and waiting for this, since it never failed.

Again and again he was bound with chains, jailed, and threatened with the sword. The photograph of this blessed individual, together with that of the great Amín, taken of them in their chains, will serve as an example to whoever has eyes to see. There they sit, those two distinguished men, hung with chains, shackled, yet composed, acquiescent, undisturbed.

Things came to such a pass that in the end whenever there was an uproar Mullá 'Alí would put on his turban, wrap himself in his 'abá and sit waiting, for his enemies to rouse and the farráshes to break in and the guards to carry him off to prison. But observe the power of God! In spite of all this, he was kept safe. "The sign of a knower and lover is this, that you will find him dry in the sea." That is how he was. His life hung by a thread from one moment to the next; the malevolent lay in wait for him; he was known everywhere as a Bahá'í—and still he was protected from all harm. He stayed dry in the depths of the sea, cool and safe in the heart of the fire, until the day he died.

After the ascension of Bahá'u'lláh, Mullá 'Alí continued on, loyal to the Testament of the Light of the World, staunch in the Covenant which he served and heralded. During the lifetime of the Manifestation, his yearning made him hasten to Bahá'u'lláh, Who received him with grace and favor, and showered blessings upon him. He returned, then, to Írán, where he devoted all his time to serving the Cause. Openly at odds with his tyrannical oppressors, no matter how often they threatened him, he defied them. He was never vanquished. Whatever he had to say, he said. He was one of the Hands of the Cause of God, steadfast, unshakable, not to be moved.

I loved him very much, for he was delightful to converse with, and as a companion second to none. One night, not long ago, I saw him in the world of dreams. Although his frame had always been massive, in the dream world he appeared larger and more corpulent than ever. It seemed as if he had returned from a journey. I said to him, "Jináb, you have grown good and stout." "Yes," he answered, "praise be to God! I have been in places where the air was fresh and sweet, and the water crystal pure; the landscapes were beautiful to look upon, the foods delectable. It all agreed with me, of course, so I am stronger than ever now, and I have recovered the zest of my early youth. The breaths of the All-Merciful blew over me and all my time was spent in telling of God. I have been setting forth His proofs, and teaching His Faith." (The meaning of teaching the Faith in the next world is spreading the sweet savors of holiness; that action is the same as teaching.) We spoke together a little more, and then some people arrived and he disappeared.

His last resting-place is in Tihrán. Although his body lies under the earth, his pure spirit lives on, "in the seat of truth, in the presence of the potent King."[3] I long to visit the graves of the friends of God, could this be possible. These are the servants of the Blessed Beauty; in His path they were afflicted; they met with toil and sorrow; they sustained injuries and suffered harm. Upon them be the glory of God, the All-Glorious. Unto them be salutation and praise. Upon them be God's tender mercy, and forgiveness.

[3] Qur'án 54:55

THE FAITHFUL

Shaykh Salmán

In 1266 A.H.[1] the trusted messenger, Shaykh Salmán, first heard the summons of God, and his heart leapt for joy. He was then in Hindíyán. Irresistibly attracted, he walked all the way to Ṭihrán, where with ardent love he secretly joined the believers. On a certain day he was passing through the bázár with Áqá Muhammad Taqíy-i-Káshání, and the farráshes followed him and discovered where he lived. The next day, police and farráshes came looking for him and took him to the chief of police.

"Who are you?" the chief asked.

"I am from Hindíyán," replied Salmán. "I have come to Ṭihrán and am on my way to Khurásán, for a pilgrimage to the Shrine of Imám Riḍá."

"What were you doing yesterday," the chief asked, "with that man in the white robe?"

Salmán answered, "I had sold him an 'abá the day before, and yesterday he was to pay me."

"You are a stranger here," the chief said. "How could you trust him?"

"A money-changer guaranteed the payment," Salmán replied. He had in mind the respected believer, Áqá Muḥammad-i-Ṣarráf (money-changer).

[1] 1849-1850.

The chief turned to one of his farráshes and said, "Take him to the money-changer's and look into it."

When they reached there the farrásh went on ahead. "What was all this," he said, "about the sale of an 'abá and your vouching for the payment? Explain yourself."

"I know nothing about it," the money-changer replied.

"Come along," said the farrásh to Salmán. "All is clear at last. You are a Bábí."

It happened that the turban which Salmán had on his head was similar to those worn in Shúshtar. As they were passing a crossroads, a man from Shúshtar came out of his shop. He embraced Salmán and cried: "Where have you been, Khájih Muḥammad-'Alí? When did you arrive? Welcome!"

Salmán replied, "I came here a few days ago and now the police have arrested me."

"What do you want with him?" the merchant asked the farrásh. "What are you after?"

"He is a Bábí," was the answer.

"God forbid!" cried the man from Shúshtar. "I know him well. Khájih Muḥammad-'Alí is a God-fearing Muslim, a Shí'ih, a devout follower of the Imám 'Alí." With this he gave the farrásh a sum of money and Salmán was freed.

They went into the shop and the merchant began to ask Salmán how he was faring. Salmán told him: "I am not Khájih Muḥammad-'Alí."

The man from Shúshtar was dumfounded. "You look exactly like him!" he exclaimed. "You two are identical. However, since you are not he, give me back the money I paid the farrásh."

Salmán immediately handed him the money, left, went out through the city gate and made for Hindíyán.

When Bahá'u'lláh arrived in 'Iráq, the first messenger to reach His holy presence was Salmán, who then returned with Tablets addressed to the friends in Hindíyán. Once each year, this blessed individual would set out on foot to see his Well-Beloved, after which he would retrace his steps, carrying Tablets to many cities, Iṣfáhán, S͟híráz, Kás͟hán, Ṭihrán, and the rest.

From the year 69 until the ascension of Bahá'u'lláh in 1309 A.H.[2], Salmán would arrive once a year, bringing letters, leaving with the Tablets, faithfully delivering each one to him for whom it was intended. Every single year throughout that long period, he came on foot from Persia to 'Iráq, or to Adrianople, or to the Most Great Prison at 'Akká; came with the greatest eagerness and love, and then went back again.

He had remarkable powers of endurance. He traveled on foot, as a rule eating nothing but onions and bread; and in all that time, he moved about in such a way that he was never once held up and never once lost a letter or a Tablet. Every letter was safely delivered; every Tablet reached its intended recipient. Over and over again, in Iṣfáhán, he was subjected to severe trials, but he remained patient and thankful under all conditions, and earned from non-Bahá'ís the title of "the Bábís' Angel Gabriel."

Throughout his entire life, Salmán rendered this momentous service to the Cause of God, becoming the means of its spread and contributing to the happiness of the believers, annually bringing Divine glad tidings to the cities and villages of Persia. He was close to the heart of Bahá'u'lláh, Who looked upon him with especial favor and grace. Among the Holy Scriptures, there are Tablets revealed in his name.

After the ascension of Bahá'u'lláh, Salmán remained faithful to the Covenant, serving the Cause with all his powers. Then, as before, he would come to the Most Great

[2] 1853; 1892.

Prison every year, delivering mail from the believers, and returning with the answers to Persia. At last, in Shíráz, he winged his way to the Kingdom of glory.

From the dawn of history until the present day, there has never been a messenger so worthy of trust; there has never been a courier to compare with Salmán. He has left respected survivors in Iṣfáhán who, because of the troubles in Persia, are presently in distress. It is certain that the friends will see to their needs. Upon him be the glory of God, the All-Glorious; unto him be salutations and praise.

Mírzá Muḥammad-'Alí, the Afnán

In the days of Bahá'u'lláh, during the worst times in the Most Great Prison, they would not permit any of the friends either to leave the Fortress or to come in from the outside. "Skew-Cap" [1] and the Siyyid [2] lived by the second gate of the city, and watched there at all times, day and night. Whenever they spied a Bahá'í traveler they would hurry away to the Governor and tell him that the traveler was bringing in letters and would carry the answers back. The Governor would then arrest the traveler, seize his papers, jail him, and drive him out. This became an estab-

[1] Áqá Ján. Cf. Shoghi Effendi, *God Passes By*, p. 189.

[2] Siyyid Muḥammad, the Antichrist of the Bahá'í Revelation. Cf. Ibid., pp. 164 and 189.

lished custom with the authorities and went on for a long time—indeed, for nine years until, little by little, the practice was abandoned.

It was at such a period that the Afnán, Ḥájí Mírzá Muḥammad-'Alí—that great bough of the Holy Tree [3]—journeyed to 'Akká, coming from India to Egypt, and from Egypt to Marseilles. One day I was up on the roof of the caravanserai. Some of the friends were with me and I was walking up and down. It was sunset. At that moment, glancing at the distant seashore, I observed that a carriage was approaching. "Gentlemen," I said, "I feel that a holy being is in that carriage." It was still far away, hardly within sight.

"Let us go to the gate," I told them. "Although they will not allow us to pass through, we can stand there till he comes." I took one or two people with me and we left.

At the city gate I called to the guard, privately gave him something and said: "A carriage is coming in and I think it is bringing one of our friends. When it reaches here, do not hold it up, and do not refer the matter to the Governor." He put out a chair for me and I sat down.

By this time the sun had set. They had shut the main gate, too, but the little door was open. The gatekeeper stayed outside, the carriage drew up, the gentleman had arrived. What a radiant face he had! He was nothing but light from head to foot. Just to look at that face made one happy; he was so confident, so assured, so rooted in his faith, and his expression so joyous. He was truly a blessed being. He was a man who made progress day by day, who added, every day, to his certitude and faith, his luminous quality, his ardent love. He made extraordinary progress during the few days that he spent in the Most Great Prison. The point is that when his carriage had come only

[3] The Afnán are the kindred of the Báb. Ibid., pp. 239; 328.

part of the way from Haifa to 'Akká, one could already perceive his spirit, his light.

After he had received the endless bounties showered on him by Bahá'u'lláh, he was given leave to go, and he traveled to China. There, over a considerable period, he spent his days mindful of God and in a manner conformable to Divine good pleasure. Later he went on to India, where he died.

The other revered Afnán and the friends in India felt it advisable to send his blessed remains to 'Iráq, ostensibly to Najaf, to be buried near the Holy City; for the Muslims had refused to let him lie in their graveyard, and his body had been lodged in a temporary repository for safekeeping. Áqá Siyyid Asadu'lláh, who was in Bombay at the time, was deputized to transport the remains with all due reverence to 'Iráq. There were hostile Persians on the steamship and these people, once they reached Búshihr, reported that the coffin of Mírzá Muḥammad-'Alí the Bábí was being carried to Najaf for burial in the Vale of Peace, near the sacred precincts of the Shrine, and that such a thing was intolerable. They tried to take his blessed remains off the ship, but they failed; see what the hidden Divine decrees can bring about.

His body came as far as Baṣra. And since that was a period when the friends had to remain in concealment, Siyyid Asadu'lláh was obliged to proceed as if he were going on with the burial in Najaf, meanwhile hoping in one way or another to effect the interment near Baghdád. Because, although Najaf is a holy city and always shall be, still the friends had chosen another place. God, therefore, stirred up our enemies to prevent the Najaf burial. They swarmed in, attacking the quarantine station to lay hold of the body and either bury it in Baṣra or throw it into the sea or out on the desert sands.

The case took on such importance that in the end it

proved impossible to bring the remains to Najaf, and Siyyid Asadu'lláh had to carry them on to Baghdád. Here, too, there was no burial place where the Afnán's body would be safe from molestation at enemy hands. Finally the Siyyid decided to carry it to the shrine of Persia's Salmán the Pure,[4] about five farsakhs out of Baghdád, and bury it in Ctesiphon, close to the grave of Salmán, beside the palace of the Sásáníyán kings. The body was taken there and that trust of God was, with all reverence, laid down in a safe resting-place by the palace of Nawshíraván.

And this was destiny, that after a lapse of thirteen hundred years, from the time when the throne city of Persia's ancient kings was trampled down, and no trace of it was left, except for rubble and hills of sand, and the very palace roof itself had cracked and split so that half of it toppled to the ground—this edifice should win back the kingly pomp and splendor of its former days. It is indeed a mighty arch. The width of its entry-way is fifty-two paces and it towers very high.

Thus did God's grace and favor encompass the Persians of an age long gone, in order that their ruined capital should be rebuilt and flourish once again. To this end, with the help of God, events were brought about which led to the Afnán's being buried here; and there is no doubt that a proud city will rise up on this site. I wrote many letters about it, until at last the holy dust could be laid to rest in this place. Siyyid Asadu'lláh would write me from Baṣra and I would answer him. One of the public functionaries there was completely devoted to us, and I directed him to do all he could. Siyyid Asadu'lláh informed me from Baghdád that he was at his wits' end, and had no idea where he could consign this body to the grave. "Wher-

[4] Herald of the Prophet Muḥammad.

ever I might bury it," he wrote, "they will dig it up again."

At last, praised be God, it was laid down in the very spot to which time and again the Blessed Beauty had repaired; in that place honored by His footsteps, where He had revealed Tablets, where the believers of Baghdád had been in His company; that very place where the Most Great Name was wont to stroll. How did this come about? It was due to the Afnán's purity of heart. Lacking this, all those ways and means could never have been brought to bear. Verily, God is the Mover of heaven and earth.

I loved the Afnán very much. Because of him, I rejoiced. I wrote a long Visitation Tablet for him and sent it with other papers to Persia. His burial site is one of the holy places where a magnificent Mashriqu'l-Adhkár must be raised up. If possible, the actual arch of the royal palace should be restored and become the House of Worship. The auxiliary buildings of the House of Worship should likewise be erected there: the hospital, the schools and university, the elementary school, the refuge for the poor and indigent; also the haven for orphans and the helpless, and the travelers' hospice.

Gracious God! That royal edifice was once splendidly decked forth and fair. But there are spiders' webs today, where hung the curtains of gold brocade, and where the king's drums beat and his musicians played, the only sound is the harsh cries of kites and crows. "This is verily the capital of the owl's realm, where thou wilt hear no sound, save only the echo of his repeated calls." That is how the barracks were, when we came to 'Akká. There were a few trees inside the walls, and on their branches, as well as up on the battlements, the owls cried all night long. How disquieting is the hoot of an owl; how it saddens the heart.

From earliest youth until he grew helpless and old, that sacred bough of the Holy Tree, with his smiling face, shone out like a lamp in the midst of all. Then he leapt and soared to undying glory, and plunged into the ocean of light. Upon him be the breathings of his Lord, the All-Merciful. Upon him, lapped in the waters of grace and forgiveness, be the mercy and favor of God.

Ḥájí Mírzá Ḥasan, the Afnán

Among the most eminent of those who left their homeland to join Bahá'u'lláh was Mírzá Ḥasan, the great Afnán, who during the latter days won the honor of emigrating and of receiving the favor and companionship of his Lord. The Afnán, related to the Báb, was specifically named by the Supreme Pen as an offshoot of the Holy Tree. When still a small child, he received his portion of bounty from the Báb, and showed forth an extraordinary attachment to that dazzling Beauty. Not yet adolescent, he frequented the society of the learned, and began to study sciences and arts. He reflected day and night on the most abstruse of spiritual questions, and gazed in wonderment at the mighty signs of God as written in the Book of Life. He became thoroughly versed even in such material sciences as mathematics, geometry, and geography; in brief, he was well grounded in many fields, thoroughly conversant with the thought of ancient and modern times.

A merchant by profession, he spent only a short period

of the day and evening at his business, devoting most of his time to discussion and research. He was truly erudite, a great credit to the Cause of God amongst leading men of learning. With a few concise phrases, he could solve perplexing questions. His speech was laconic, but in itself a kind of miracle.

Although he first became a believer in the days of the Báb, it was during the days of Bahá'u'lláh that he caught fire. Then his love of God burned away every obstructing veil and idle thought. He did all he could to spread the Faith of God, becoming known far and wide for his ardent love of Bahá'u'lláh.

I am lost, O Love, possessed and dazed,
Love's fool am I, in all the earth.
They call me first among the crazed,
Though I once came first for wit and worth . . .

After the ascension of the Báb, he had the high honor of serving and watching over the revered and saintly consort of the blessed Lord. He was in Persia, mourning his separation from Bahá'u'lláh, when his distinguished son became, by marriage, a member of the Holy Household. At this, the Afnán rejoiced. He left Persia and hastened to the sheltering favor of his Well-Beloved. He was a man amazing to behold, his face so luminous that even those who were not believers used to say that a heavenly light shone from his forehead.

He went away for a time and sojourned in Beirut, where he met the noted scholar, K͟hájih Findík. This personage warmly praised the erudition of the great Afnán in various circles, affirming that an individual of such wide and diverse learning was rare throughout the East. Later on, the Afnán returned to the Holy Land, settling near the Mansion of Bahjí and directing all his thoughts toward aspects of human culture. Much of the time he would occupy himself with uncovering the secrets of the heavens, contemplating in their detail the movements of the stars. He had a telescope with which he would make his observations every night. He lived a happy life, carefree and light of heart. In the neighborhood of Bahá'u'lláh his days were blissful, his nights bright as the first morning in spring.

But then came the Beloved's departure from this world. The Afnán's peace was shattered, his joy was changed to grief. The Supreme Affliction was upon us, separation consumed us, the once bright days turned black as night, and all those roses of other hours were dust and rubble now. He lived on for a little while, his heart smoldering, his eyes shedding their tears. But he could not bear the longing for his Well-Beloved, and in a little while his soul gave up this life and fled to the eternal one; passed into the Heaven of abiding reunion and was immersed beneath an ocean of light. Upon him be most great mercy, plenteous bounty, and every blessing, as the ages and cycles roll on. His honored tomb is in 'Akká at the Mans͟híyyih.

Muḥammad-'Alíy-i-Iṣfáhání

Muhammad-'Ali of Iṣfáhán was among the earliest of believers, guided to the Faith from its very beginning. He was one of the mystics; his house was a gathering place for them, and the philosophers. Noble, high-minded, he was one of Iṣfáhán's most respected citizens, and served as a host and sanctuary for every stranger, rich or poor. He had verve, an excellent disposition, was forbearing, affable, generous, a boon companion; and it was known throughout the city that he enjoyed a good time.

Then he was led to embrace the Faith and caught fire from the Sinaitic Tree. His house became a teaching center, dedicated to the glory of God. Day and night the believers flocked there, as to a lamp lit by heavenly love. Over a long period, the sacred verses were chanted in that house and the clear proofs set forth. Although this was widely known, Muḥammad-'Alí was not molested, because he was a kinsman of the Imám-Jum'ih of Iṣfáhán. Finally, however, things came to such a pass that the Imám-Jum'ih himself sent him away, telling him: "I can protect you no longer. You are in grave danger. The best thing for you is to leave here, and go on a journey."

He left his home then, went to 'Iráq, and entered the presence of the world's Desired One. He spent some time there, progressing every day; he had little to live on, but was happy and content. A man of excellent disposition, he was cogenial to believers and others alike.

When Bahá'u'lláh and His retinue left Baghdád for Constantinople, Muḥammad-'Alí was in His company, and continued on with Him to the Land of Mystery, Adrianople. Not one to be inconstant, he maintained his characteristic immutability of heart. Whatever happened, he remained the same. In Adrianople as well, his days passed happily, under the protection of Bahá'u'lláh. He would carry on some business which, however trifling, would bring in surprisingly abundant returns.

From Adrianople, Muḥammad-'Alí accompanied Bahá'u'lláh to the fortress of 'Akká, was put in jail there, and was numbered among Bahá'u'lláh's fellow captives for the rest of his life, achieving that greatest of all distinctions, to be in prison with the Blessed Beauty.

He spent his days in utter bliss. Here, too, he carried on a small business, which occupied him from morning till noon. In the afternoons he would take his samovar, wrap it in a dark-colored pouch made from a saddlebag, and go off somewhere to a garden or meadow, or out in a field, and have his tea. Sometimes he would be found at the farm of Mazra'ih, or again in the Riḍván Garden; or, at the Mansion, he would have the honor of attending upon Bahá'u'lláh.

Muḥammad-'Alí would carefully consider every blessing that came his way. "How delicious my tea is today," he would comment. "What perfume, what color! How lovely this meadow is, and the flowers so bright!" He used to say that everything, even air and water, had its own special fragrance. For him the days passed in indescribable delight. Even kings were not so happy as this old man, the people said. "He is completely free of the world," they would declare. "He lives in joy." It also happened that his food was of the very best, and that his home was situated in the very best part of 'Akká. Gracious God! Here he was, a prisoner, and yet experiencing comfort, peace and joy.

Muḥammad-'Alí was past eighty when he finally departed to eternal light. He had been the recipient of many Tablets from Bahá'u'lláh, and of endless bounty, under all conditions. Upon him be the glory of God the Most Glorious. Upon him be myriads of heavenly blessings; may God favor him with gladness forever and ever. His luminous grave is in 'Akká.

'Abdu's-Ṣáliḥ, the Gardener

AMONG THOSE who emigrated and were companions in the Most Great Prison was Áqá 'Abdu's-Ṣáliḥ. This excellent soul, a child of early believers, came from Iṣfáhán. His noble-hearted father died, and this child grew up an orphan. There was none to rear or care for him and he was the prey of anyone who chose to do him harm. At last he became adolescent, and older now, sought out his Well-Beloved. He emigrated to the Most Great Prison and here, at the Riḍván, achieved the honor of being appointed gardener. At this task he was second to none. In his faith, too, he was staunch, loyal, worthy of trust; as to his character, he was an embodiment of the sacred verse, "Of a noble nature art thou." [1] That is how he won the distinction of being gardener at the Riḍván, and of thus receiving the greatest bounty of all: almost daily, he entered the presence of Bahá'u'lláh.

For the Most Great Name was held prisoner and confined nine years in the fortress-town of 'Akká; and at all times, both in the barracks and afterward, from without the house, the police and farráshes had Him under constant guard. The Blessed Beauty lived in a very small house,

[1] Qur'án 68:4.

and He never set foot outside that narrow lodging, because His oppressors kept continual watch at the door. When, however, nine years had elapsed, the fixed and predetermined length of days was over; and at that time, against the rancorous will of the tyrant, 'Abdu'l-Ḥamíd, and all his minions, Bahá'u'lláh proceeded out of the fortress with authority and might, and in a kingly mansion beyond the city, made His home.

Although the policy of Sulṭán 'Abdu'l-Ḥamíd was harsher than ever; although he constantly insisted on his Captive's strict confinement—still, the Blessed Beauty now lived, as everyone knows, with all power and glory. Some of the time Bahá'u'lláh would spend at the Mansion, and again, at the farm village of Mazra'ih; for a while He would sojourn in Haifa, and occasionally His tent would be pitched on the heights of Mount Carmel. Friends from everywhere presented themselves and gained an audience. The people and the government authorities witnessed it all, yet no one so much as breathed a word. And this is one of Bahá'u'lláh's greatest miracles: that He, a captive, surrounded Himself with panoply and He wielded power. The prison changed into a palace, the jail itself became a Garden of Eden. Such a thing has not occurred in history before; no former age has seen its like: that a man confined to a prison should move about with authority and might; that one in chains should carry the fame of the Cause of God to the high heavens, should win splendid victories in both East and West, and should, by His almighty pen, subdue the world. Such is the distinguishing feature of this supreme Theophany.

One day the government leaders, pillars of the country, the city's 'ulamás, leading mystics and intellectuals came out to the Mansion. The Blessed Beauty paid them no attention whatever. They were not admitted to His presence, nor did He inquire after any of them. I sat down with them and kept them company for some hours, after which they returned whence they had come. Although the royal farmán specifically decreed that Bahá'u'lláh was to be held in solitary confinement within the 'Akká fortress, in a cell, under perpetual guard; that He was never to set foot outside; that He was never even to see any of the believers—notwithstanding such a farmán, such a drastic order, His tent was raised in majesty on the heights of Mount Carmel. What greater display of power could there be than this, that from the very prison, the banner of the Lord was raised aloft, and rippled out for all the world to see! Praised be the Possessor of such majesty and might; praised be He, weaponed with the power and the glory; praised be He, Who defeated His foes when He lay captive in the 'Akká prison!

To resume: 'Abdu'ṣ-Ṣáliḥ lived under a fortunate star, for he regularly came into the presence of Bahá'u'lláh. He enjoyed the distinction of serving as gardener for many years, and he was at all times loyal, true, and strong in faith. He was humble in the presence of every one of the believers; in all that time he never hurt nor offended any one. And at the last he left his garden and hastened to the encompassing mercy of God.

The Ancient Beauty was well pleased with 'Abdu'ṣ-Ṣáliḥ, and after his ascension revealed a Visitation Tablet in his honor, also delivering an address concerning him, which was taken down and published together with other Scriptures.

Upon him be the glory of the All-Glorious! Upon him be God's gentleness and favor in the Exalted Realm.

Ustád Ismá'íl

Yet another from amongst that blessed company was Ustád Ismá'íl, the builder. He was the construction overseer of Farrukh Khán (Amínu'd-Dawlih) in Ṭihrán, living happily and prosperously, a man of high standing, well regarded by all. But he lost his heart to the Faith, and was enraptured by it, till his holy passion consumed every intervening veil. Then he cast caution aside, and became known throughout Ṭihrán as a pillar of the Bahá'ís.

Farrukh Khán ably defended him at first. But as time went on, he summoned him and said, "Ustád, you are very dear to me and I have given you my protection and have stood by you as best I could. But the Sháh has found out about you and you know what a bloodthirsty tyrant he is. I am afraid that he will seize you without warning, and he will hang you. The best thing for you is to go on a journey. Leave this country, go somewhere else, and escape from this peril."

Composed, happy, Ustád gave up his work, closed his eyes to his possessions, and left for 'Iráq, where he lived in poverty. He had recently taken a bride, and loved her beyond measure. Her mother arrived, and by subterfuge, obtained his permission to conduct the daughter back to Ṭihrán, supposedly for a visit. As soon as she reached

Kirmánsháh, she went to the mujtahid, and told him that because her son-in-law had abandoned his religion, her daughter could not remain his lawful wife. The mujtahid arranged a divorce, and wedded the girl to another man. When word of this reached Baghdád, Ismá'íl, steadfast as ever, only laughed. "God be praised!" he said. "Nothing is left me on this pathway. I have lost everything, including my bride. I have been able to give Him all I possessed."

When Bahá'u'lláh departed from Baghdád, and traveled to Rumelia, the friends remained behind. The inhabitants of Baghdád then rose up against those helpless believers, sending them away as captives to Mosul. Ustád was old and feeble, but he left on foot, with no provisions for his journey, crossed over mountains and deserts, valleys and hills, and in the end arrived at the Most Great Prison. At one time, Bahá'u'lláh had written down an ode of Rúmí's for him, and had told him to turn his face toward the Báb and sing the words, set to a melody. And so as he wandered through the long dark nights, Ustád would sing these lines:

I am lost, O Love, possessed and dazed,
Love's fool am I, in all the earth.
They call me first among the crazed,
Though I once came first for wit and worth.

O Love, who sellest me this wine,[1]
O Love, for whom I burn and bleed,
Love, for whom I cry and pine—
Thou the Piper, I the reed.

[1] This wine, Rúmí says elsewhere, comes from the jar of "Yea verily." That is, it symbolizes the Primal Covenant established between God and man on the day of "Am I not your Lord?" On that day, the Creator summoned posterity out of the loins of Adam and said to the generations unborn, "Am I not your Lord?" Whereupon they answered, "Yea, verily, Thou art." Cf. Qur'án 7:171.

THE FAITHFUL

If Thou wishest me to live,
Through me blow Thy holy breath.
The touch of Jesus Thou wilt give
To me, who've lain an age in death.

Thou, both End and Origin,
Thou without and Thou within—
From every eye Thou hidest well,
And yet in every eye dost dwell.

He was like a bird with broken wings but he had the song and it kept him going onward to his one true Love. By stealth, he approached the Fortress and went in, but he was exhausted, spent. He remained for some days, and came into the presence of Bahá'u'lláh, after which he was directed to look for a lodging in Haifa. He got himself to Haifa, but he found no haven there, no nest or hole, no water, no grain of corn. Finally he made his home in a cave outside the town. He acquired a little tray and on this he set out rings of earthenware, and some thimbles, pins and other trinkets. Every day, from morning till noon, he peddled these, wandering about. Some days his earnings would amount to twenty paras,[2] some days thirty; and forty on his best days. Then he would go home to the cave and content himself with a piece of bread. He was always voicing his thanks, always saying, "Praise be to God that I have attained such favor and grace; that I have been separated from friend and stranger alike, and have taken refuge in this cave. Now I am of those who gave their all, to buy the Divine Joseph in the market place. What bounty could be any greater than this!"

Such was his condition, when he died. Many and many a time, Bahá'u'lláh was heard to express His satisfaction

[2] The Turkish para was one-ninth of a cent. Cf. Webster, *New International Dictionary.*

with Ustád Ismá'íl. Blessings hemmed him round, and the eye of God was on him. Salutations be unto him, and praise. Upon him be the glory of the All-Glorious.

Nabíl-i-Zarandí

STILL ANOTHER of those who emigrated from their native land to be near Bahá'u'lláh was the great Nabíl.[1] In the flower of youth he bade farewell to his family in Zarand and with Divine aid began to teach the Faith. He became a chief of the army of lovers, and on his quest he left Persian 'Iráq for Mesopotamia, but could not find the One he sought. For the Well-Beloved was then in Kurdistán, living in a cave at Sar-Galú; and there, entirely alone in that wasteland, with no companion, no friend, no listening soul, He was communing with the beauty that dwelt in His own heart. All news of Him was completely cut off; 'Iráq was eclipsed, and in mourning.

When Nabíl discovered that the flame which had once been kindled and tended there was almost out, that the believers were few, that Yaḥyá[2] had crawled into a secret

[1] Nabíl, author of *The Dawn-Breakers,* is Bahá'u'lláh's "Poet-Laureate, His chronicler and His indefatigable disciple." Cf. *God Passes By,* p. 130.

[2] Mírzá Yaḥyá, the community's "nominal head," was the "center provisionally appointed pending the manifestation of the Promised One." Ibid., p. 127-28.

hole where he lay torpid and inert, and that a wintry cold had taken over—he found himself obliged to leave, bitterly grieving, for Karbilá. There he stayed until the Blessed Beauty returned from Kurdistán, making His way to Baghdád. At that time there was boundless joy; every believer in the country sprang to life; among them was Nabíl, who hastened to the presence of Bahá'u'lláh, and became the recipient of great bestowals. He spent his days in gladness now, writing odes to celebrate the praises of his Lord. He was a gifted poet, and his tongue most eloquent; a man of mettle, and on fire with passionate love.

After a time he returned to Karbilá, then came back to Baghdád and from there went on to Persia. Because he associated with Siyyid Muḥammad he was led into error and sorely afflicted and tried; but like the shooting stars, he became as a missile to drive off satanic imaginings,[3] and he repulsed the evil whisperers and went back to Baghdád, where he found rest in the shade of the Holy Tree. He was later directed to visit Kirmánsháh. He returned again, and on every journey was enabled to render a service.

Bahá'u'lláh and His retinue then left Baghdád, the "Abode of Peace," for Constantinople, the "City of Islám." After His departure, Nabíl put on the dress of a dervish, and set out on foot, catching up with the convoy along the way. In Constantinople he was directed to return to Persia and there teach the Cause of God; also to travel throughout the country, and acquaint the believers in its cities and villages with all that had taken place. When this mission was accomplished, and the drums of "Am I not your Lord?" were rolling out—for it was the "year eighty"[4]—

[3] A reference to Islámic symbolism, according to which good is protected from evil: the angels repel such evil spirits as attempt to spy on Paradise, by hurling shooting stars at them. Cf. Qur'án 15:18, 37:10 and 67:5.

[4] A reference to the declaration of Bahá'u'lláh's advent in 1863, as the Promised One of the Báb. The Báb's own advent had taken place in the "year sixty"—1844.

Nabíl hurried to Adrianople, crying as he went, "Yea verily Thou art! Yea verily!" and "Lord, Lord, here am I!"

He entered Bahá'u'lláh's presence and drank of the red wine of allegiance and homage. He was then given specific orders to travel everywhere, and in every region to raise the call that God was now made manifest: to spread the blissful tidings that the Sun of Truth had risen. He was truly on fire, driven by restive love. With great fervor he would pass through a country, bringing this best of all messages and reviving the hearts. He flamed like a torch in every company, he was the star of every assemblage, to all who came he held out the intoxicating cup. He journeyed as to the beat of drums and at last he reached the 'Akká fortress.

In those days the restrictions were exceptionally severe. The gates were shut, the roads closed off. Wearing a disguise, Nabíl arrived at the 'Akká gate. Siyyid Muḥammad and his wretched accomplice immediately hurried to the Governorate and informed against the traveler. "He is a Persian," they reported. "He is not, as he seems, a man of Bukhárá. He has come here to seek for news of Bahá'u'lláh." The authorities expelled him at once.

Nabíl, despairing, withdrew to the town of Ṣafad. Later he came on to Haifa, where he made his home in a cave on Mount Carmel. He lived apart from friend and stranger alike, lamenting night and day, moaning and chanting prayers. There he remained as a recluse, and waited for the doors to open. When the predestined time of captivity was over, and the gates were flung wide, and the Wronged One issued forth in beauty, in majesty and glory, Nabíl hastened to Him with a joyful heart. Then he used himself up like a candle, burning away with the love of God. Day and night he sang the praises of the one Beloved of both worlds and of those about His threshold, writing verses in the pentameter and hexameter forms, composing lyrics and long odes. Almost daily, he was admitted to the presence of the Manifestation.[5]

This went on until the day Bahá'u'lláh ascended. At that supreme affliction, that shattering calamity, Nabíl sobbed and trembled and cried out to Heaven. He found that the numerical value of the word "s͟hidád"—year of stress—was 309, and it thus became evident that Bahá'u'lláh foretold what had now come to pass.[6]

Utterly cast down, hopeless at being separated from Bahá'u'lláh, fevered, shedding tears, Nabíl was in such anguish that anyone seeing him was bewildered. He struggled on, but the only desire he had was to lay down his life. He could suffer no longer; his longing was aflame in him; he could stand the fiery pain no more. And so he became king of the cohorts of love, and he rushed into the sea.

Before that day when he offered himself up, he wrote out the year of his death in the one word: "Drowned." [7] Then he threw down his life for the Well-Beloved, and was released from his despair, and no longer shut away.

This distinguished man was erudite, wise, and eloquent of speech. His native genius was pure inspiration, his poetic gift like a crystal stream. In particular his ode "Bahá, Bahá!" was written in sheer ecstasy. Throughout all his life, from earliest youth till he was feeble and old, he spent

[5] Bahá'í writings emphasize that the "divinity attributed to so great a Being and the complete incarnation of the names and attributes of God in so exalted a Person should, under no circumstances, be misconceived or misinterpreted . . . that invisible yet rational God . . . however much we extol the divinity of His Manifestations on earth, can in no wise incarnate His infinite, His unknowable, His incorruptible and all-embracing Reality in . . . a mortal being." Cf. Shoghi Effendi, *The Dispensation of Bahá'u'lláh.*

[6] According to the abjad reckoning, the letters of "s͟hidád" total 309. 1892, the date of Bahá'u'lláh's ascension, was 1309 A.H.

[7] G͟haríq. The letters composing this word total 1310, which Hijra year began July 26, 1892.

his time serving and worshiping the Lord. He bore hardships, he lived through misfortunes, he suffered afflictions. From the lips of the Manifestation he heard marvelous things. He was shown the lights of Paradise; he won his dearest wish. And at the end, when the Daystar of the world had set, he could endure no more, and flung himself into the sea. The waters of sacrifice closed over him; he was *drowned,* and he came, at last, to the Most High.

Upon him be abundant blessings; upon him be tender mercies. May he win a great victory, and a manifest grace in the Kingdom of God.

Darvís͟h Ṣidq-'Alí

ÁQÁ ṢIDQ-'ALÍ was yet one more of those who left their native land, journeyed to Bahá'u'lláh and were put in the Prison. He was a dervish; a man who lived free and detached from friend and stranger alike. He belonged to the mystic element and was a man of letters. He spent some time wearing the dress of poverty, drinking the wine of the Rule and traveling the Path,[1] but unlike the other Ṣúfís he did not devote his life to dusty ḥas͟hísh; on the contrary, he cleansed himself of their vain imaginings and only searched for God, spoke of God, and followed the path of God.

[1] Terms used by the Ṣúfís.

THE FAITHFUL

He had a fine poetic gift and wrote odes to sing the praises of Him Whom the world has wronged and rejected. Among them is a poem written while he was a prisoner in the barracks at 'Akká, the chief couplet of which reads:

A hundred hearts Thy curling locks ensnare,
And it rains hearts when Thou dost toss Thy hair.

That free and independent soul discovered, in Baghdád, a trace of the untraceable Beloved. He witnessed the dawning of the Daystar above the horizon of 'Iráq, and received the bounty of that sunrise. He came under the spell of Bahá'u'lláh, and was enraptured by that tender Companion. Although he was a quiet man, one who held his peace, his very limbs were like so many tongues crying out their message. When the retinue of Bahá'u'lláh was about to leave Baghdád he implored permission to go along as a groom. All day, he walked beside the convoy, and when night came he would attend to the horses. He worked with all his heart. Only after midnight would he seek his bed and lie down to rest; the bed, however, was his mantle, and the pillow a sun-dried brick.

As he journeyed, filled with yearning love, he would sing poems. He greatly pleased the friends. In him the name [2] bespoke the man: he was pure candor and truth; he was love itself; he was chaste of heart, and enamored of Bahá'u'lláh. In his high station, that of groom, he reigned like a king; indeed he gloried over the sovereigns of the earth. He was assiduous in attendance upon Bahá'u'lláh; in all things, upright and true.

The convoy of the lovers went on; it reached Constantinople; it passed to Adrianople, and finally to the 'Akká

[2] Ṣidq, truth.

prison. Ṣidq-'Alí was present throughout, faithfully serving its Commander.

While in the barracks, Bahá'u'lláh set apart a special night and He dedicated it to Darvísh Ṣidq-Alí. He wrote that every year on that night the dervishes should bedeck a meeting place, which should be in a flower garden, and gather there to make mention of God. He went on to say that "dervish" does not denote those persons who wander about, spending their nights and days in fighting and folly; rather, He said, the term designates those who are completely severed from all but God, who cleave to His laws, are firm in His Faith, loyal to His Covenant, and constant in worship. It is not a name for those who, as the Persians say, tramp about like vagrants, are confused, unsettled in mind, a burden to others, and of all mankind the most coarse and rude.

This eminent dervish spent his whole life-span under the sheltering favor of God. He was completely detached from worldly things. He was attentive in service, and waited upon the believers with all his heart. He was a servant to all of them, and faithful at the Holy Threshold.

Then came that hour when, not far from his Lord, he stripped off the cloak of life, and to physical eyes passed into the shadows, but to the mind's eye betook himself to what is plain as day; and he was seated there on a throne of lasting glory. He escaped from the prison of this world, and pitched his tent in a wide and spacious land. May God ever keep him close and bless him in that mystic realm with perpetual reunion and the beatific vision; may he be wrapped in tiers of light. Upon him be the glory of God, the All-Glorious. His grave is in 'Akká.

Áqá Mírzá Maḥmúd and Áqá Riḍá

These two blessed souls, Mírzá Maḥmúd of Ká<u>sh</u>án and Áqá Riḍá of <u>Sh</u>íráz, were like two lamps lit with God's love from the oil of His knowledge. Encompassed by Divine bestowals from childhood on, they succeeded in rendering every kind of service for fifty-five years. Their services were countless, beyond recording.

When the retinue of Bahá'u'lláh left Ba<u>gh</u>dád for Constantinople, He was accompanied by a great crowd of people. Along the way, they met with famine conditions. These two souls strode along on foot, ahead of the howdah in which Bahá'u'lláh was riding, and covered a distance of seven or eight farsa<u>kh</u>s every day. Wayworn and faint, they would reach the halting-place; and yet, weary as they were, they would immediately set about preparing and cooking the food, and seeing to the comfort of the believers. The efforts they made were truly more than flesh can bear. There were times when they had not more than two or three hours sleep out of the twenty-four; because, once the friends had eaten their meal, these two would be busy collecting and washing up the dishes and cooking utensils; this would take them till midnight, and only then would they rest. At daybreak they would rise, pack everything, and set out again, in front of the howdah of Bahá'u'-

lláh. See what a vital service they were able to render, and for what bounty they were singled out: from the start of the journey, at Baghdád, to the arrival in Constantinople, they walked close beside Bahá'u'lláh; they made every one of the friends happy; they brought rest and comfort to all; they prepared whatever anyone asked.

Áqá Riḍá and Mírzá Maḥmúd were the very essence of God's love, utterly detached from all but God. In all that time no one ever heard either of them raise his voice. They never hurt nor offended anyone. They were trustworthy, loyal, true. Bahá'u'lláh showered blessings upon them. They were continually entering His presence and He would be expressing His satisfaction with them.

Mírzá Maḥmúd was a youth when he arrived in Baghdád from Ká<u>sh</u>án. Áqá Riḍá became a believer in Baghdád. The spiritual condition of the two was indescribable. There was in Baghdád a company of seven leading believers who lived in a single, small room, because they were destitute. They could hardly keep body and soul together, but they were so spiritual, so blissful, that they thought themselves in Heaven. Sometimes they would chant prayers all night long, until the day broke. Days, they would go out to work, and by nightfall one would have earned ten paras, another perhaps twenty paras, others forty or fifty. These sums would be spent for the evening meal. On a certain day one of them made twenty paras, while the rest had nothing at all. The one with the money bought some dates, and shared them with the others; that was dinner, for seven people. They were perfectly content with their frugal life, supremely happy.

These two honored men devoted their days to all that is best in human life: they had seeing eyes; they were mindful and aware; they had hearing ears, and were fair of speech. Their sole desire was to please Bahá'u'lláh. To them, nothing was a bounty at all, except service at His

Holy Threshold. After the time of the Supreme Affliction, they were consumed with sorrow, like candles flickering away; they longed for death, and stayed firm in the Covenant and labored hard and well to spread that Daystar's Faith. They were close and trusted companions of 'Abdu'l-Bahá, and could be relied on in all things. They were always lowly, humble, unassuming, evanescent. In all that long period, they never uttered a word which had to do with self.

And at the last, during the absence of 'Abdu'l-Bahá, they took their flight to the Kingdom of unfading glory. I sorrowed much because I was not with them when they died. Although absent in body, I was there in my heart, and mourning over them; but to outward seeming I did not bid them good-by; this is why I grieve.

Unto them both be salutations and praise; upon them be compassion and glory. May God give them a home in Paradise, under the Lote-Tree's shade. May they be immersed in tiers of light, close beside their Lord, the Mighty, the All-Powerful.

Pidar-Ján of Qazvín

THE LATE Pidar-Ján was among those believers who emigrated to Baghdád. He was a godly old man, enamored of the Well-Beloved; in the garden of Divine love, he was like a rose full-blown. He arrived there, in Baghdád, and spent his days and nights communing with God and chanting prayers; and although he walked the earth, he traveled the heights of Heaven.

To obey the law of God, he took up a trade, for he had nothing. He would bundle a few pairs of socks under his arm and peddle them as he wandered through the streets and bázárs, and thieves would rob him of his merchandise. Finally he was obliged to lay the socks across his outstretched palms as he went along. But he would get to chanting a prayer, and one day he was surprised to find that they had stolen the socks, laid out on his two hands, from before his eyes. His awareness of this world was clouded, for he journeyed through another. He dwelt in ecstasy; he was a man drunken, bedazzled.

For some time, that is how he lived in 'Iráq. Almost daily he was admitted to the presence of Bahá'u'lláh. His name was 'Abdu'lláh but the friends bestowed on him the title of Pidar-Ján—Father Dear—for he was a loving father to them all. At last, under the sheltering care of Bahá'u'lláh, he took flight to the "seat of truth, in the presence of the potent king."[1]

May God make fragrant his sepulcher with the outpouring rains of His mercy and cast upon him the eye of Divine compassion. Salutations be unto him, and praise.

[1] Qur'án 54:55

Shaykh Ṣádiq-i-Yazdí

ANOTHER of those who emigrated to Baghdád was Shaykh Ṣádiq of Yazd, a man esteemed, and righteous as his name, Ṣádiq.[1] He was a towering palm in the groves of Heaven, a star flaming in the skies of the love of God.

It was during the 'Iráq period that he hastened to the presence of Bahá'u'lláh. His detachment from the things of this world and his attachment to the life of the spirit are indescribable. He was love embodied, tenderness personified. Day and night, he commemorated God. Utterly unconscious of this world and all that is therein, he dwelt continually on God, remaining submerged in supplications and prayers. Most of the time, tears poured from his eyes. The Blessed Beauty singled him out for special favor, and whenever He turned His attention toward Ṣádiq, His loving-kindness was clear to see.

On a certain day they brought word that Ṣádiq was at the point of death. I went to his bedside and found him breathing his last. He was suffering from ileus, an abdominal pain and swelling. I hurried to Bahá'u'lláh and described his condition.

[1] This word has a number of meanings, including truthful, loyal and just.

"Go," He said. "Place your hand on the distended area and speak the words: 'O Thou the Healer!' "[2]

I went back. I saw that the affected part had swollen up to the size of an apple; it was hard as stone, in constant motion, twisting, and coiling about itself like a snake. I placed my hand upon it; I turned toward God and, humbly beseeching Him, I repeated the words, "O Thou the Healer!" Instantly the sick man rose up. The ileus vanished; the swelling was carried off.

This personified spirit lived contentedly in 'Iráq until the day when Bahá'u'lláh's convoy wended its way out of Baghdád. As bidden, Ṣádiq remained behind in that city. But his longing beat so passionately within him that after the arrival of Bahá'u'lláh at Mosul, he could endure the separation no more. Shoeless, hatless, he ran out alongside the courier going to Mosul; ran and ran until, on that barren plain, with mercy all about him, he fell to his rest.

May God give him to drink from "a wine cup tempered at the camphor fountain,"[3] and send down crystal waters on his grave; may God perfume his dust in that desert place with musk, and cause to descend there range on range of light.

[2] Yá Sháfí.
[3] Qur'án 76:5.

Sh̲áh-Muḥammad-Amín

Sh̲áh-Muḥammad, who had the title of Amín, the Trusted One, was among the earliest of believers, and most deeply enamored. He had listened to the Divine summons in the flower of his youth, and set his face toward the Kingdom. He had ripped from his gaze the veils of idle suppositions and had won his heart's desire; neither the fancies current among the people nor the reproaches of which he was the target turned him back. Unshaken, he stood and faced a sea of troubles; staunch with the strength of the Advent day, he confronted those who tried to thwart him and block his path. The more they sought to instill doubts in his mind, the stronger he became; the more they tormented him, the more progress he made. He was a captive of the face of God, enslaved by the beauty of the All-Glorious; a flame of God's love, a jetting fountain of the knowledge of Him.

Love smoldered in his heart, so that he had no peace; and when he could bear the absence of the Beloved One no more, he left his native home, the province of Yazd. He found the desert sands like silk under his feet; light as the wind's breath, he passed over the mountains and across the endless plains, until he stood at the door of his

Love. He had freed himself from the snare of separation, and in 'Iráq, he entered the presence of Bahá'u'lláh.

Once he made his way into the home of the Darling of mankind, he was emptied of every thought, released from every concern, and became the recipient of boundless favor and grace. He passed some days in 'Iráq and was directed to return to Persia. There he remained for a time, frequenting the believers; and his pure breathings stirred each one of them anew, so that each one yearned over the Faith, and became more restless, more impatient than before.

Later he arrived at the Most Great Prison with Mírzá Abu'l-Ḥasan, the second Amín. On this journey he met with severe hardships, for it was extremely difficult to find a way into the prison. Finally he was received by Bahá'u'lláh in the public baths. Mírzá Abu'l-Ḥasan was so overwhelmed at the majestic presence of his Lord that he shook, stumbled, and fell to the floor; his head was injured and the blood flowed out.

Amín, that is S͟háh-Muḥammad, was honored with the title of the Trusted One, and bounties were showered upon him. Full of eagerness and love, taking with him Tablets from Bahá'u'lláh, he hastened back to Persia, where, at all times worthy of trust, he labored for the Cause. His services were outstanding, and he was a consolation to the believers' hearts. There was none to compare with him for energy, enthusiasm and zeal, and no man's services could equal his. He was a haven amidst the people, known everywhere for devotion to the Holy Threshold, widely acclaimed by the friends.

He never rested for a moment. Not one night did he spend on a bed of ease, never did he lay down his head on comfort's pillow. He was continuously in flight, soaring as the birds do, running like a deer, guesting in the desert of oneness, alone and swift. He brought joy to all the believers; to all, his coming was good news; to every seeker, he was a sign and token. He was enamored of God, a vagrant in the desert of God's love. Like the wind, he traveled over the face of the plains, and he was restive on the heights of the hills. He was in a different country every day, and in yet another land by nightfall. Never did he rest, never was he still. He was forever rising up to serve.

But then they took him prisoner in Ádhirbáyján, in the town of Míyándu'áb. He fell a prey to some ruthless Kurds, a hostile band who asked no questions of the innocent, defenseless man. Believing that this stranger, like other foreigners, wished ill to the Kurdish people, and taking him for worthless, they killed him.

When news of his martyrdom reached the Prison, all the captives grieved, and they shed tears for him, resigned to God and undefended as he was in his last hour. Even on the countenance of Bahá'u'lláh, there were visible tokens of grief. A Tablet, infinitely tender, was revealed by the Supreme Pen, commemorating the man who died on that calamitous plain, and many other Tablets were sent down concerning him.

Today, under the shadowing mercy of God, he dwells in the bright Heavens. He communes with the birds of holiness, and in the assemblage of splendors he is immersed in light. The memory and praise of him shall remain, till the end of time, in the pages of books and on the tongues and lips of men.

Unto him be salutations and praise; upon him be the glory of the All-Glorious; upon him be the most great mercy of God.

Mas͟hhadí Fatṭáḥ

Mas͟hhadí Fatṭáḥ was personified spirit. He was devotion itself. Brother to Ḥájí 'Alí-'Askar—of the same pure lineage—through the latter he came into the Faith. Like the twins, Castor and Pollux, the two kept together in one spot, and both were illumined with the light of belief.

In all things, the two were united as a pair; they shared the same certitude and faith, the same conscience, and made their way out of Ád͟hirbáyján to Adrianople, emigrating at the same time. In every circumstance of their life, they lived as one individual; their disposition, their aims, their religion, character, behavior, faith, certitude, knowledge—all were one. Even in the Most Great Prison, they were constantly together.

Mas͟hhadí Fatṭáḥ possessed some merchandise; this was all he owned in the world. He had entrusted it to persons in Adrianople, and later on those unrighteous people did away with the goods. Thus, in the pathway of God, he lost whatever he possessed. He passed his days, perfectly content, in the Most Great Prison. He was utter selflessness; from him, no one ever heard a syllable to indicate that he existed. He was always in a certain corner of the prison, silently meditating, occupied with the remembrance of God; at all times spiritually alert and mindful, in a state of supplication.

Then came the Supreme Affliction. He could not tolerate the anguish of parting with Bahá'u'lláh, and after Bahá'u'lláh's passing, he died of grief. Blessed is he; again, blessed is he. Glad tidings to him; again, glad tidings to him. Upon him be the glory of the All-Glorious.

Nabíl of Qá'in

THIS DISTINGUISHED man, Mullá Muḥammad-'Alí,[1] was one of those whose hearts were drawn to Bahá'u'lláh before the Declaration of the Báb; it was then that he drank the red wine of knowledge from the hands of the Cupbearer of grace. It happened that a prince, who was the son of Mír Asadu'lláh K͟hán, prince of Qá'in, was commanded to remain as a political hostage in Ṭihrán. He was young, far away from his loving father, and Mullá Muḥammad-'Alí was his tutor and guardian. Since the youth was a stranger in Ṭihrán, the Blessed Beauty showed him special kindness. Many a night the young prince was Bahá'u'lláh's guest at the mansion, and Mullá Muḥammad-'Alí would accompany him. This was prior to the Declaration of the Báb.

[1] Nabíl of Qá'in was his title.

It was then that this chief of all trusted friends was captivated by Bahá'u'lláh, and wherever he went, spread loving praise of Him. After the way of Islám, he also related the great miracles which he had, with his own eyes, seen Bahá'u'lláh perform, and the marvels he had heard. He was in ecstasy, burning up with love. In that condition, he returned to Qá'in with the prince.

Later on that eminent scholar, Áqá Muḥammad of Qá'in (whose title was Nabíl-i-Akbar) was made a mujtahid, a doctor of religious law, by the late Shaykh Murtaḍá; he left, then, for Baghdád, became an ardent follower of Bahá'u'lláh, and hastened back to Persia. The leading divines and mujtahids were well aware of and acknowledged his vast scholarly accomplishments, the breadth of his learning, and his high rank. When he reached Qá'in, he began openly to spread the new Faith. The moment Mullá Muḥammad-'Alí heard the name of the Blessed Beauty, he immediately accepted the Báb. "I had the honor," he said, "of meeting the Blessed Beauty in Ṭihrán. The instant I saw Him, I became His slave."

In his village of Sar-Cháh, this gifted, high-minded man began to teach the Faith. He guided in his own family and saw to the others as well, bringing a great multitude under the law of the love of God, leading each one to the path of salvation.

Up to that time he had always been a close companion of Mír 'Alam Khán, the Governor of Qá'in, had rendered him important services, and had enjoyed the Governor's respect and trust. Now that shameless prince turned against him in a rage on account of his religion, seized his property and plundered it; for the Amír was terrified of Náṣiri'd-Dín Sháh. He banished Nabíl-i-Akbar and ruined Nabíl of Qá'in. After throwing him in prison and torturing him, he drove him out as a homeless vagrant.

To Nabíl, the sudden calamity was a blessing, the sacking of his earthly goods, the expulsion into the desert, was a kingly crown and the greatest favor God could grant him. For some time he remained in Ṭihrán, to outward seeming a pauper of no fixed abode, but inwardly rejoicing; for this is the characteristic of every soul who is firm in the Covenant.

He had access to the society of the great and knew the condition of the various princes. He would, therefore, frequent some of them and give them the message. He was a consolation to the hearts of the believers and as a drawn sword to the enemies of Bahá'u'lláh. He was one of those of whom we read in the Qur'án: "For the Cause of God shall they strive hard; the blame of the blamer shall they not fear."[2] Day and night he toiled to promote the Faith, and with all his might to spread abroad the clear signs of God. He would drink and drink again of the wine of God's love, was clamorous as the storm clouds, restless as the waves of the sea.

Permission came, then, for him to visit the Most Great Prison; for in Ṭihrán, as a believer, he had become a marked man. They all knew of his conversion; he had no caution, no patience, no reserve; he cared nothing for reticence, nothing for dissimulation. He was utterly fearless and in terrible danger.

When he arrived at the Most Great Prison, the hostile watchers drove him off, and try as he might he found no way to enter. He was obliged to leave for Nazareth, where he lived for some time as a stranger, alone with his two sons, Áqá Qulám-Ḥusayn and Áqá 'Alí-Akbar, grieving and praying. At last a plan was devised to introduce him into the fortress and he was summoned to the prison where they had immured the innocent. He came in such ecstasy as cannot be described, and was admitted to the presence of

[2] Qur'án 5:59.

Bahá'u'lláh. When he entered there and lifted his eyes to the Blessed Beauty he shook and trembled and fell unconscious to the floor. Bahá'u'lláh spoke words of loving-kindness to him and he rose again. He spent some days hidden in the barracks, after which he returned to Nazareth.

The inhabitants of Nazareth wondered much about him. They told one another that he was obviously a great and distinguished man in his own country, a notable and of high rank; and they asked themselves why he should have chosen such an out-of-the-way corner of the world as Nazareth and how he could be contented with such poverty and hardship.

When, in fulfillment of the promise of the Most Great Name, the gates of the Prison were flung wide, and all the friends and travelers could enter and leave the fortress-town in peace and with respect, Nabíl of Qá'in would journey to see Bahá'u'lláh once in every month. However, as commanded by Him, he continued to live in Nazareth, where he converted a number of Christians to the Faith; and there he would weep, by day and night, over the wrongs that were done to Bahá'u'lláh.

His means of livelihood was his business partnership with me. That is, I provided him with a capital of three krans;[3] with it he bought needles, and this was his stock-in-trade. The women of Nazareth gave him eggs in exchange for his needles and in this way he would obtain thirty or forty eggs a day: three needles per egg. Then he would sell the eggs and live on the proceeds. Since there was a daily caravan between 'Akká and Nazareth, he would refer to Áqá Riḍá each day, for more needles. Glory be to God! He survived two years on that initial outlay of capital; and he returned thanks at all times. You can tell

[3] The kran was 20 s͟háhís, or almost 8 cents. Cf. Webster, op. cit.

how detached he was from worldly things by this one fact: the Nazarenes used to say it was plain to see from the old man's manner and behavior that he was very rich, and that if he lived so modestly it was only because he was a stranger in a strange place—hiding his wealth by setting up as a peddler of needles.

Whenever he came into the presence of Bahá'u'lláh he received still more evidences of favor and love. For all seasons, he was a close friend and companion to me. When sorrows attacked me I would send for him, and then I would rejoice just to see him again. How wonderful his talk was, how attractive his society. Bright of face he was; free of heart; loosed from every earthly tie, always on the wing. Toward the end he made his home in the Most Great Prison, and every day he entered the presence of Bahá'u'lláh.

On a certain day, walking through the bázár with his friends, he met a gravedigger named Ḥájí Aḥmad. Although in the best of health, he addressed the gravedigger and laughingly told him: "Come along with me." Accompanied by the believers and the gravedigger he made for Nabíyu'lláh Ṣáliḥ. Here he said: "O Ḥájí Aḥmad, I have a request to make of you: when I move on, out of this world and into the next, dig my grave here, beside the Purest Branch.[4] This is the favor I ask." So saying, he gave the man a gift of money.

That very evening, not long after sunset, word came that Nabíl of Qá'in had been taken ill. I went to his home at once. He was sitting up, and conversing. He was radiant, laughing, joking, but for no apparent reason the sweat was pouring off his face—it was rushing down. Except for this

[4] Mírzá Mihdí, the son of Bahá'u'lláh who, praying one evening on the barracks roof, fell to his death. Cf. *God Passes By,* p. 188.

he had nothing the matter with him. The perspiring went on and on; he weakened, lay in his bed, and toward morning, died.

Bahá'u'lláh would refer to him with infinite grace and loving-kindness, and revealed a number of Tablets in his name. The Blessed Beauty was wont, after Nabíl's passing, to recall that ardor, the power of that faith, and to comment that here was a man who had recognized Him, prior to the advent of the Báb.

All hail to him for this wondrous bestowal. "Blessedness awaiteth him and a goodly home . . . And God will single out for His mercy whomsoever He willeth."[5]

Siyyid Muḥammad-Taqí Man<u>sh</u>ádí

Muḥammad-Taqí came from the village of Man<u>sh</u>ád. When still young, he learned of the Faith of God. In holy ecstasy, his mind turned Heavenward, and his heart was flooded with light. Divine grace descended upon him; the summons of God so enraptured him that he threw the peace of Man<u>sh</u>ád to the winds. Leaving his kinsfolk and children, he set out over mountains and desert plains, passed from one halting-place to the next, came to the seashore, crossed over the sea and at last reached the

[5] Cf. Qur'án 13:28; 2:99; 3:67.

city of Haifa. From there he hastened on to 'Akká and entered the presence of Bahá'u'lláh.

In the early days he opened a small shop in Haifa and carried on some trifling business. God's blessing descended upon it, and it prospered. That little corner became the haven of the pilgrims. When they arrived, and again at their departure, they were guests of the high-minded and generous Muḥammad-Taqí. He also helped to manage the affairs of the believers, and would get together their means of travel. He proved unfailingly reliable, loyal, worthy of trust. Ultimately he became the intermediary through whom Tablets could be sent away and mail from the believers could come in. He performed this service with perfect dependability, accomplishing it in a most pleasing way, scrupulously despatching and receiving the correspondence at all times. Trusted by everyone, he became known in many parts of the world, and received unnumbered bounties from Bahá'u'lláh. He was a treasury of justice and righteousness, entirely free from any attachment to worldly things. He had accustomed himself to a very spare way of life, caring nothing for food or sleep, comfort or peace. He lived all alone in a single room, passed the nights on a couch of palm branches, and slept in a corner. But to the travelers, he was a spring in the desert; for them, he provided the softest of pillows, and the best table he could afford. He had a smiling face and by nature was spiritual and serene.

After the Daystar of the Supreme Concourse had set, Siyyid Man<u>sh</u>ádí remained loyal to the Covenant, a sharp sword confronting the violators. They tried every ruse, every deceit, all their subtlest expedients; it is beyond imagining how they showered favors on him and what honors they paid him, what feasts they prepared, what pleasures they offered, all this to make a breach in his faith. Yet every day he grew stronger than before, continued to be staunch and true, kept free from every unseemly thought, and shunned whatever went contrary to the Covenant of God. When they finally despaired of shaking his resolve, they harassed him in every possible way, and plotted his financial ruin. He remained, however, the quintessence of constancy and trust.

When, at the instigation of the violators, 'Abdu'l-Ḥámíd began his opposition to me, I was obliged to send Man<u>sh</u>ádí away to Port Saïd, because he was widely known among the people as the distributor of our mail. I then had to relay the correspondence to him through intermediaries who were unknown, and he would send the letters on as before. In this way the treacherous and the hostile were unable to take over the mail. During the latter days of 'Abdu'l-Ḥámíd, when a commission of investigation appeared and—urged on by those familiars-turned-strangers—made plans to tear out the Holy Tree by the roots; when they determined to cast me into the depths of the sea or banish me to the Fezzan, and this was their settled purpose; and when the commission accordingly tried their utmost to get hold of some document or other, they failed. In the thick of all that turmoil, with all the pressures and restraints, and the foul attacks of those persons who were pitiless as Yazíd,[1] still the mail went through.

For many long years, Siyyid Man<u>sh</u>ádí befittingly performed this service in Port Saïd. The friends were uniformly pleased with him. In that city he earned the gratitude of travelers, placed those who had emigrated in his debt, brought joy to the local believers. Then the heavy heat of Egypt proved too much for him; he took to his bed,

[1] Yazíd (son of Mu'áviyyih), 'Ummayad Caliph by whose order the Imám Ḥusayn was martyred. Proverbial for cruelty. Cf. S. Haïm, *New Persian-English Dictionary*, s.v.

and in a raging fever, cast off the robe of life. He abandoned Port Saïd for the Kingdom of Heaven, and rose up to the mansions of the Lord.

Siyyid Manshádí was the essence of virtue and intellect. His qualities and attainments were such as to amaze the most accomplished minds. He had no thought except of God, no hope but to win the good pleasure of God. He was the embodiment of "Make all my song one single praise of Thee; forever keep me faithful in Thy service."

May God cool his feverish pain with the grace of reunion in the Kingdom, and heal his sickness with the balm of nearness to Him in the Realm of the All-Beauteous. Upon him be the glory of God the Most Glorious.

Muḥammad-'Alí Ṣabbáq of Yazd

Early in youth, Muḥammad-'Alí Ṣabbáq became a believer while in 'Iráq. He tore away hindering veils and doubts, escaped from his delusions and hastened to the welcoming shelter of the Lord of Lords. A man to outward seeming without education, for he could neither read nor write, he was of sharp intelligence and a trustworthy friend. Through one of the believers, he was brought into the presence of Bahá'u'lláh, and was soon widely known to the public as a disciple. He found himself a corner to live in, close beside the house of the Blessed Beauty, and mornings and evenings would enter the presence of Bahá'u'lláh. For a time he was supremely happy.

When Bahá'u'lláh and His retinue left Baghdád for Constantinople, Áqá Muḥammad-'Alí was of that company, and fevered with the love of God. We reached Constantinople; and since the Government obliged us to settle in Adrianople we left Muḥammad-'Alí in the Turkish capital to assist the believers as they came and went through that city. We then went on to Adrianople. This man remained alone and he suffered intense distress for he had no friend nor companion nor anyone to care for him.

After two years of this he came on to Adrianople, seeking a haven in the loving-kindness of Bahá'u'lláh. He went to work as a peddler, and when the great rebellion [1] began and the oppressors drove the friends to the extreme of adversity, he too was among the prisoners and was exiled with us to the fortress at 'Akká.

He spent a considerable time in the Most Great Prison, after which Bahá'u'lláh desired him to leave for Sidon, where he engaged in trade. Sometimes he would return and be received by Bahá'u'lláh, but otherwise he stayed in Sidon. He lived respected and trusted, a credit to all. When

[1] The rebellion of Mírzá Yaḥyá, who had been named provisional chief of the Bábí community. The Báb had never appointed a successor or viceregent, instead referring His disciples to the imminent advent of His Promised One. In the interim a virtual unknown was, for security reasons, made the ostensible leader. Following His declaration in 1863 as the Promised One of the Báb, Bahá'u'lláh withdrew for a time, in Adrianople, to allow the exiles a free choice as between Him and this unworthy half brother, whose crimes and follies had threatened to destroy the infant Faith. Terrified at being challenged to face Bahá'u'lláh in a public debate, Mírzá Yaḥyá refused, and was completely discredited. As Bahá'í history has repeatedly demonstrated, this crisis too, however grievous, resulted in still greater victories for the Faith—including the rallying of prominent disciples to Bahá'u'lláh, and the global proclamation of Bahá'u'lláh's mission, in His Tablets to the Pope and Kings. Cf. *God Passes By,* p. 28, Chapter X and passim.

the Supreme Affliction came upon us, he returned to 'Akká and passed the remainder of his days near the Holy Tomb.

The friends, one and all, were pleased with him, and he was cherished at the Holy Threshold; in this state he soared to abiding glory, leaving his kin to mourn. He was a kind man, an excellent one: content with God's will for him, thankful, a man of dignity, long-suffering. Upon him be the glory of the All-Glorious. May God send down, upon his scented tomb in 'Akká, tiers of celestial light.

'Abdu'l-G͟haffár of Iṣfáhán

ANOTHER of those who left their homeland to become our neighbors and fellow prisoners was 'Abdu'l-G͟haffár of Iṣfáhán. He was a highly perceptive individual who, on commercial business, had traveled about Asia Minor for many years. He made a journey to 'Iráq, where Áqá Muḥammad-'Alí of Ṣád (Iṣfáhán) brought him into the shelter of the Faith. He soon ripped off the bandage of illusions that had blinded his eyes before, and he rose up, winging to salvation in the Heaven of Divine love. With him, the veil had been thin, almost transparent, and that is why, as the first word was imparted, he was immediately released from the world of idle imaginings and attached himself to the One Who is clear to see.

On the journey from 'Iráq to the Great City, Constantinople, 'Abdu'l-Ghaffár was a close and agreeable companion. He served as interpreter for the entire company, for he spoke excellent Turkish, a language in which none of the friends was proficient. The journey came peacefully to an end and then, in the Great City, he continued on, as a companion and friend. The same was true in Adrianople and also when, as one of the prisoners, he accompanied us to the city of Haifa.

Here, the oppressors determined to send him to Cyprus. He was terrified and shouted for help, for he longed to be with us in the Most Great Prison.[1] When they held him back by force, from high up on the ship he threw himself into the sea. This had no effect whatever on the brutal officers. After dragging him from the water they held him prisoner on the ship, cruelly restraining him, and carrying him away by force to Cyprus. He was jailed in Famagusta, but one way or another managed to escape and hastened to 'Akká. Here, protecting himself from the malevolence of our oppressors, he changed his name to 'Abdu'lláh. Sheltered within the loving-kindness of Bahá'u'lláh, he passed his days at ease, and happy.

But when the world's great Light had set, to shine on forever from the All-Luminous Horizon, 'Abdu'l-Ghaffár was beside himself and a prey to anguish. He no longer had a home. He left for Damascus and spent some time there, pent up in his sorrow, mourning by day and night. He grew weaker and weaker. We despatched Ḥájí 'Abbás there, to nurse him and give him treatment and care, and send back word of him every day. But 'Abdu'l-Ghaffár would do nothing but talk, unceasingly, at every hour,

[1] Mírzá Yaḥyá had not been banished from Persia. Now, however, he was being exiled from Adrianople to Cyprus, and 'Abdu'l-Ghaffár was one of the four companions condemned to go with him. Cf. Bahá'u'lláh's *Epistle to the Son of the Wolf,* p. 166, and *God Passes By,* p. 182.

with his nurse, and tell how he longed to go his way, into the mysterious country beyond. And at the end, far from home, exiled from his Love, he set out for the Holy Threshold of Bahá'u'lláh.

He was truly a man long-suffering, and mild; a man of good character, good acts, and goodly words. Greetings and praise be unto him, and the glory of the All-Glorious. His sweet-scented tomb is in Damascus.

'Alí Najaf-Ábádí

ALSO AMONG the emigrants and near neighbors was Áqá 'Alí Najaf-Ábádí. When this spiritual young man first listened to the call of God he set his lips to the holy cup and beheld the glory of the Speaker on the Mount. And when, by grace of the light, he had attained positive knowledge, he journeyed to the Most Great Prison, where he witnessed the substance of knowledge itself, and arrived at the high station of indubitable truth.

For a long time he remained in and about the sacred city; he became the proverbial Ḥabíbu'lláh the Merchant, and spent his days relying upon God, in supplication and prayer. He was a man meek, quiet, uncomplaining, steadfast; in all things pleasing, worthy of praise. He won the approval of all the friends and was accepted and welcome at the Holy Threshold. During his latter days, when he felt that a happy end was in store for him, he again presented himself at the holy city of the Most Great Prison. Upon arrival he fell ill, weakened, passed his hours in supplicating God. The breath of life ceased within him, the gates of flight to the supreme Kingdom were flung wide, he turned his eyes away from this world of dust and went onward to the Holy Place.

'Alí Najaf-Ábádí was tender and sensitive of heart, at all times mindful of God and remembering Him, and toward the close of his life detached, without stain, free from the contagion of this world. Sweetly, he gave up his corner of the earth, and pitched his tent in the land beyond. May God send upon him the pure savors of forgiveness, brighten his eyes with beholding the Divine Beauty in the Kingdom of Splendors, and refresh his spirit with the musk-scented winds that blow from the Abhá Realm. Unto him be salutation and praise. His sweet and holy dust lies in 'Akká.

Ma<u>sh</u>hadí Ḥusayn and Ma<u>sh</u>hadí Muḥammad-i-Á<u>dh</u>irbáyjání

Ma<u>sh</u>hadí Ḥusayn and Ma<u>sh</u>hadí Muḥammad were both from the province of Á<u>dh</u>irbáyján. They were pure souls who took the great step in their own country:

they freed themselves from friend and stranger alike, escaped from the superstitions that had blinded them before, strengthened their resolve, and bowed themselves down before the grace of God, the Lord of Life. They were blessed souls, loyal, unsullied in faith; evanescent, submissive, poor, content with the will of God, in love with His guiding Light, rejoicing over the great message. They left their province and traveled to Adrianople. Here beside the holy city they lived for quite a time in the village of Qumruq-Kilísá. By day, they supplicated God and communed with Him; by night, they wept, bemoaning the plight of Him Whom the world hath wronged.

When the exile to 'Akká was under way, they were not present in the city and thus were not arrested. Heavy of heart, they continued on in that area, shedding their tears. Once they had obtained a definite report from 'Akká, they left Rumelia and came here: two excellent souls, loyal bondsmen of the Blessed Beauty. It is impossible to tell how translucent they were of heart, how firm in faith.

They lived outside 'Akká in Bágh-i-Firdaws, worked as farmers, and spent their days returning thanks to God because once again they had won their way to the neighborhood of grace and love. But they were natives of Ádhirbáyján, accustomed to the cold, and they could not endure the local heat. Furthermore, this was during our early days in 'Akká, when the air was noxious, and the water unwholesome in the extreme. They both fell ill of a chronic, high fever. They bore it cheerfully, with amazing patience. During their days of illness, despite the assault of the fever, the violence of their ailment, the raging thirst, the restlessness, they remained inwardly at peace, rejoicing at the Divine glad tidings. And at a time when they were offering thanks with all their heart, they hurried away from this world and entered the other; they escaped from this cage and were released into the garden of immortality. Upon them be the mercy of God, and may He be well pleased with them. Unto them be salutations and praise. May God bring them into the Realm that abides forever, to delight in reunion with Him; to bask in the Kingdom of Splendors. Their two luminous tombs are in 'Akká.

Ḥájí 'Abdu'r-Raḥím-i-Yazdí

Ḥájí 'Abdu'r-Raḥím of Yazd was a precious soul, from his earliest years virtuous and God-fearing, and known among the people as a holy man, peerless in observing his religious duties, mindful as to his acts. His strong religious faith was an indisputable fact. He served and worshiped God by day and night, was sound, mild, compassionate, a loyal friend.

Because he was fully prepared, at the very moment when he heard the summons from the Supreme Horizon—heard the drumbeats of "Am I not your Lord?"—he instantly cried out, "Yea, verily!" With his whole being, he became enamored of the splendors shed by the Light of the World. Openly and boldly he began to confirm his family and friends. This was soon known throughout the city; to the eyes of the evil 'ulamás, he was now an object of hate and contempt. Incurring their wrath, he was despised by those creatures of their own low passions. He was molested and harassed; the inhabitants rioted, and the evil 'ulamás plotted his death. The government authorities turned on him as well, hounded him, even subjected him to torture. They beat him with clubs, and whipped him. All this went on, by day and night.

He was forced, then, to abandon his home and go out of the city, a vagrant, climbing the mountains, crossing over the plains, until he came to the Holy Land. But so weak he was, and wasted away, that whoever saw him thought he was breathing his last; when he reached Haifa, Nabíl of Qá'in hurried to 'Akká, and desired me to summon the Ḥájí at once, because he was in his death agony and failing fast.

"Let me go to the Mansion," I said, "and ask leave."

"It would take too long," he said. "And then 'Abdu'r-Raḥím will never see 'Akká. I long for him to have this bounty; for him at least to see 'Akká, and die. I beg of You, send for him at once!"

Complying with his wish, I summoned 'Abdu'r-Raḥím. When he came, I could hardly detect in him a whisper of life. At times he would open his eyes, but he spoke no word. Still, the sweet savors of the Most Great Prison restored the vital spark, and his yearning to meet Bahá'u'lláh breathed life into him again. I looked in on him the next morning and found him cheerful and refreshed. He asked permission to attend upon Bahá'u'lláh. "It all depends," I answered, "on whether He grants you leave. God willing, you shall be singled out for this cherished gift."

A few days later, permission came, and he hastened to the presence of Bahá'u'lláh. When 'Abdu'r-Raḥím entered there, the spirit of life was wafted over him. On his return, it was clear that this Ḥájí had become a different Ḥájí entirely: he was in the bloom of health. Nabíl was dumfounded, and said: "How life-giving, to a true believer, is this prison air!"

For some time, 'Abdu'r-Raḥím lived in the neighborhood. He spent his hours remembering and praising God; he chanted prayers, and carefully attended to his religious duties. Thus he saw few people. This servant paid special attention to his needs, and ordered a light diet for him. But it all came to an end with the Supreme Affliction, the ascension of Bahá'u'lláh. There was anguish then, and the noise of loud weeping. With his heart on fire, his eyes raining tears, he struggled weakly to move about; so his days went by, and always, he longed to make his exit from this rubbish heap, the world. At last he broke away from the torment of his loss, and hurried on to the Realm of God, and came to the assemblage of Divine splendor in the Kingdom of Lights.

Unto him be salutations and praise, and mercy ineffable. May God scatter on his resting-place rays from the mysterious Realm.

Ḥájí 'Abdu'lláh Najaf-Ábádí

Once he had become a believer, Ḥájí 'Abdu'lláh left his native Persia, hastened to the Holy Land, and under the sheltering grace of Bahá'u'lláh found peace of heart. He was a man confident, steadfast and firm; certain of the manifold bounties of God; of an excellent disposition and character.

He spent his days in friendly association with the other

believers. Then for a while he went to Ghawr, near Tiberias, where he farmed, both tilling the soil and devoting much of his time to supplicating and communing with God. He was an excellent man, high-minded and unsullied.

Later he returned from Ghawr, settled near Bahá'u'lláh in Junayna, and came often into His presence. His eyes were fixed on the Abhá Kingdom; sometimes he would shed tears and moan, again he would rejoice, glad because he had achieved his supreme desire. He was completely detached from all but God, happy in God's grace. He would keep a vigil most of the night, remaining in a state of prayer. Then death came at the appointed hour, and in the shadowing care of Bahá'u'lláh he ascended, hurried away from this world of dust to the high Firmament, soared upward to the secret land. Unto him be salutations, mercy and praise, in the neighborhood of his exalted Lord.

Muḥammad-Hádíy-i-Ṣaḥḥáf

YET ONE more among those who emigrated and came to settle near Bahá'u'lláh was the bookbinder, Muḥammad-Hádí. This noted man was from Iṣfáhán, and as a binder and illuminator of books he had no peer. When he gave himself up to the love of God he was alert on the path and fearless. He abandoned his home and began a dreadful journey, passing with extreme hardship from one country to another until he reached the Holy Land and became a prisoner. He stationed himself by the Holy Threshold, carefully sweeping it and keeping watch. Through his constant efforts, the square in front of Bahá'u'lláh's house was at all times swept, sprinkled and immaculate.

Bahá'u'lláh would often glance at that plot of ground, and then He would smile and say: "Muḥammad-Hádí has turned the square in front of this prison into the bridal-bower of a palace. He has brought pleasure to all the neighbors and earned their thanks."

When his sweeping, sprinkling and tidying was done, he would set to work illuminating and binding the various books and Tablets. So his days went by, his heart happy in the presence of the Beloved of mankind. He was an excellent soul, righteous, true, worthy of the bounty of being united with his Lord, and free of the world's contagion.

One day he came to me and complained of a chronic ailment. "I have suffered from chills and fever for two years," he said, "The doctors have prescribed a purgative, and quinine. The fever stops a few days; then it returns. They give me more quinine, but still the fever returns. I am weary of this life, and can no longer do my work. Save me!"

"What food would you most enjoy?" I asked him. "What would you eat with great appetite?"

"I don't know," he said.

Jokingly, I named off the different dishes. When I came to barley soup with whey (á<u>sh</u>-i-ka<u>sh</u>k), he said, "Very good! But on condition there is braised garlic in it."

I directed them to prepare this for him, and I left. The next day he presented himself and told me: "I ate a whole bowlful of the soup. Then I laid my head on my pillow and slept peacefully till morning."

In short, from then on he was perfectly well for about two years.

One day a believer came to me and said: "Muḥammad-Hádí is burning up with fever." I hurried to his bedside and found him with a fever of 42° Centigrade. He was barely conscious. "What has he done?" I asked. "When he became feverish," was the reply, "he said that he knew from experience what he should do. Then he ate his fill of barley soup with whey and braised garlic; and this was the result."

I was astounded at the workings of fate. I told them: "Because, two years ago, he had been thoroughly purged and his system was clear; because he had a hearty appetite for it, and his ailment was fever and chills, I prescribed the barley soup. But this time, with the different foods he has had, with no appetite, and especially with a high fever, there was no reason to diagnose the previous chronic condition. How could he have eaten the soup!" They answered, "It was fate." Things had gone too far; Muḥammad-Hádí was past saving.

He was a man short of stature, lofty of station and mind. His heart was pure, his soul luminous. During all those days when he served the Holy Threshold, he was loved by the friends and favored by God. From time to time, a smile on His lips, the Blessed Beauty would speak to him, expressing kindness and grace.

Muḥammad-Hádí was loyal always, and he accounted all things other than God's good pleasure as fiction and fable, nothing more. Blessed is he for this gift bestowed upon him, glad tidings to him for the place to which he shall be led; may it do him good, this wine-cup tempered at the camphor fountain, and may all his strivings meet with thanks and be acceptable to God.[1]

[1] Cf. Qur'án 11:101; 11:100; 76:5; 76:22; 17:20.

Mírzá Muḥammad-Qulí

JINÁB-I-MÍRZÁ MUḤAMMAD-QULÍ[1] was a loyal brother of the Blessed Beauty. This great man was known even from his childhood for nobility of soul. He was newly born when his distinguished father passed away, and thus it came about that from the beginning to the end of his days, he spent his life in the sheltering arms of Bahá'u'lláh. He was detached from every selfish thought, averse to every mention except to whatever concerned the Holy Cause. He was reared in Persia under the care of Bahá'u'lláh, and in 'Iráq as well, especially favored by Him. In the presence of Bahá'u'lláh, it was he who would pass around the tea; and he waited upon his Brother at all times, by day and night. He was always silent. He always held fast to the Covenant of "Am I not your Lord?" He was encompassed by loving-kindness and bounty; day and night he had access to the presence of Bahá'u'lláh; he was invariably patient and forbearing, until in the end he reached the very heights of Divine favor and acceptance.

He kept always to his own way of being. He traveled in the company of Bahá'u'lláh; from 'Iráq to Constantinople

[1] Cf. *God Passes By,* p. 108.

he was with the convoy and at the halting-places it was his task to pitch the tents. He served with the greatest diligence, and did not know the meaning of lethargy or fatigue. In Constantinople as well, and later in the Land of Mystery, Adrianople, he continued on, in one and the same invariable condition.

With his peerless Lord, he then was exiled to the 'Akká fortress, condemned by order of the Sulṭán to be imprisoned forever.[2] But he accepted in the same spirit all that came his way—comfort and torment, hardship and respite, sickness and health; eloquently, he would return thanks to the Blessed Beauty for His bounties, uttering praise with a free heart and a face that shone like the sun. Each morning and evening he waited upon Bahá'u'lláh, delighting in and sustained by His presence; and mostly, he kept silent.

When the Beloved of all mankind ascended to the Kingdom of Splendors, Mírzá Muḥammad-Qulí remained firm in the Covenant, shunning the craft, the malice and hypocrisy which then appeared, devoting himself entirely to God, supplicating and praying. To those who would listen he gave wise advice; and he called to mind the days of the Blessed Beauty and grieved over the fact that he himself lived on. After the departure of Bahá'u'lláh, he did not draw an easeful breath; he kept company with no one, but stayed by himself most of the time, alone in his small refuge, burning with the fires of separation. Day by day he grew feebler, more helpless, until at the last he soared away to the world of God. Upon him be peace; upon him be praise and mercy, in the gardens of Heaven. His luminous grave is in Naqíb, by Tiberias.

[2] Cf. *God Passes By,* pp. 186; 193; 196.

Ustád Báqir and Ustád Aḥmad

AND AGAIN among those who left their homeland were two carpenters, Ustád Báqir and Ustád Aḥmad. These two were brothers, of pure lineage, and natives of Káshán. From the time when both became believers each held the other in his embrace. They harkened to the voice of God, and to His cry of "Am I not your Lord?" they replied, "Yea, verily!"

For a time they stayed on in their own country, occupied with the remembrance of God, characterized by faith and knowledge, respected by friend and stranger alike, known to all for righteousness and trustworthiness, for austerity of life and the fear of God. When the oppressor stretched forth his hands against them, and tormented them beyond endurance, they emigrated to 'Iráq, to the sheltering care of Bahá'u'lláh. They were two most blessed souls. For some time they remained in 'Iráq, praying in all lowliness, and supplicating God.

Then Ustád Aḥmad departed for Adrianople, while Ustád Báqir remained in 'Iráq and was taken as a prisoner to Mosul. Ustád Aḥmad went on with the party of Bahá'u'lláh to the Most Great Prison, and Ustád Báqir emigrated from Mosul to 'Akká. Both of the brothers were under the protection of God and free from every earthly bond. In the prison, they worked at their craft, keeping to themselves, away from friend and stranger alike. Tranquil, dignified, confident, strong in faith, sheltered by the All-Merciful, they happily spent their days. Ustád Báqir was the first to die, and some time afterward his brother followed him.

These two were firm believers, loyal, patient, at all times thankful, at all times supplicating God in lowliness, with their faces turned in His direction. During that long stay in the prison they were never neglectful of duty, never at fault. They were constantly joyful, for they had drunk deep of the holy cup; and when they soared upward, out of the world, the friends mourned over them and asked that by the grace of Bahá'u'lláh, they should be favored and forgiven. These two were embosomed in bounty, and Divinely sustained, and the Blessed Beauty was well pleased with them both; with this provision for their journey, they set out for the world to come. Upon them both be the glory of God the All-Glorious; to each be a seat of truth [1] in the Kingdom of Splendors.

Muḥammad Ḥaná-Sáb

This man of dignity and rank, Áqá Muḥammad, was yet another among those who abandoned their homes, and was one of the earliest believers. From the dawn tide, he was widely known as a lover of the Most Great Light.

[1] Qur'án 54:55.

He was then in Iṣfáhán, and he shut his eyes to this world and the next as well,[1] and opened them to the beauty of Him Who is the embodiment of all that is lovable.[2]

Áqá Muḥammad could no longer find rest, for he had come alive through the musk-laden breathings of God; his heart was alight, he could inhale the holy fragrance, he had an eye to see, an ear to hear. He guided a number of souls, remaining true and loyal to the great Cause. He endured terrible persecution and torment, but did not falter. Then he found favor in the eyes of the King of Martyrs and became a trusted attendant of the Beloved of Martyrs,[3] serving them for some years. He was confirmed in his work, so that on many occasions the King of Martyrs expressed satisfaction with him, saying, "This man is one of those souls who are at rest; he is indeed well-pleased with his Lord, and well-pleasing unto Him.[4] His faith is unalloyed, he loves God, he has a good character, and leads a good life. He is also an agreeable companion, and an eloquent one."

After the King of Martyrs was put to death, Áqá Muḥammad stayed on for a time in Iṣfáhán, consumed with mourning for him. Finally he emigrated to the Most Great Prison, where he was received by Bahá'u'lláh, and won the high honor of sweeping the ground about the Threshold. He was patient, forbearing, a true friend and companion. Then the Supreme Affliction came upon us, and

[1] This reference to two worlds, *du jihán,* may indicate the saying: Iṣfáhán is half the world—*Iṣfáhán niṣf-i-jihán.*

[2] For this definition of the Manifestation of God, see *God Passes By,* p. 119.

[3] These "twin shining lights" were two brothers, famous merchants of Iṣfáhán. Because he owed them a large sum of money, the leading priest—Imám Jum'ih—of the city brought about their martyrdom. See Bahá'u'lláh's *Epistle to the Son of the Wolf,* and *God Passes By,* pp. 200-201 and 219.

[4] Qur'án 89: 27-30.

Áqá Muḥammad was in such anguish that he was unable to rest for a moment. At every dawn he would rise and would sweep the ground about the house of Bahá'u'lláh, his tears pouring down like rain, chanting prayers as he worked.

What a holy being he was, how great a man! He could not bear the separation very long, but died, and hastened onward to the world of lights, to the assemblage where the beauty of God is unveiled. May God shed upon his grave rays from the realm of forgiveness, and lull his spirit in the heart of Paradise. May God exalt his station in the gardens above. His bright tomb is in 'Akká.

Ḥájí Faraju'lláh Tafrísh͟í

YET ANOTHER of those who came out of their homeland to live in the neighborhood of Bahá'u'lláh was Faraju'lláh of Tafrísh͟. This blessed individual was from earliest youth the servant of Bahá'u'lláh, and with his esteemed father, Áqá Luṭfu'lláh, he emigrated from Persia to Adrianople. Áqá Luṭfu'lláh was a staunch believer, lovingly devoted to the Blessed Beauty. Patient, long-suffering, completely indifferent to this world and its vanities, he lived content in the neighborhood of Bahá'u'lláh; and then humbly at the Threshold, with a contrite heart, he abandoned this fleeting life and soared away to the boundless realms beyond. His sweet-scented dust is in Adrianople.

As for Ḥájí Faraju'lláh, he lived on in that city, until the day when merciless oppressors banished Bahá'u'lláh to 'Akká, and in His company the Ḥájí came here to the Most Great Prison. Later on, when hardship was changed into ease, he engaged in trade, becoming a partner to Muḥammad-'Alí of Iṣfáhán. For some time he prospered and was happy. Then he was given leave to go, and journeyed to India, where he spent a long period before he winged his way into the gardens of forgiveness, and entered the precincts of ineffable mercy.

This servant of the Blessed Beauty was one with the believers in their afflictions and calamities; he had his share of the anguish. The favors of Bahá'u'lláh compassed him about, and he rejoiced in that boundless grace. He was among the companions, a close associate of the friends, and he had a docile heart. Although his body was thin and sickly, he was thankful, accepted it, was patient, and endured the trials of God's path. Unto him be greetings and praise; may he receive Heavenly gifts and blessings; upon him be the glory of God the All-Glorious. His pure sepulcher is in Bombay, India.

THE FAITHFUL

Áqá Ibráhím-i-Iṣfáhání and His Brothers

AND AMONG those who emigrated and came to settle in the Holy Land was Áqá Ibráhím, one of four honored brothers: Muḥammad-Ṣádiq; Muḥammad-Ibráhím; Áqá Ḥabíbu'lláh; and Muḥammad-'Alí. These four lived in Ba<u>gh</u>dád with their paternal uncle, Áqá Muḥammad-Riḍá, known as 'Aríḍ. They all lived in the same house, and remained together day and night. Bird-like, they shared the one nest; and they were always fresh and full of grace, like flowers in a bed.

When the Ancient Beauty arrived in 'Iráq their house was in the neighborhood of His, and thus they had the joy of watching Him as He came and went. Little by little the manner of that Lord of hearts, what He did and what He did not do, and the sight of His lovesome face, had its effect; they began to thirst after the Faith and to seek His grace and favor. They presented themselves at the door of His house, as if they were flowers blooming there; and they were soon enamored of the light that shone out from His brow, captives of the beauty of that dear Companion. They needed no teacher, then; by themselves, they saw through the veils that had blinded them before, and won the supreme desire of their hearts.

As commanded by the Blessed Beauty, Mírzá Javád of

Tur<u>sh</u>íz went to their house one night. Mírzá Javád had hardly opened his mouth when they accepted the Faith. They did not hesitate for an instant, for they had amazing receptivity. This is what is meant by the Qur'ánic verse: ". . . whose oil would well nigh shine out, even though fire touched it not! It is light upon light." [1] That is, this oil is so fully prepared, so ready to be lit, that it almost catches fire of itself, though no flame be at hand; which means that the capacity for faith, and the deserving it, can be so great, that without the communication of a single word the light shines forth. This is how it was with those pure-hearted men; truly they were loyal, staunch, and devoted to God.

The eldest brother, Muḥammad-Ṣádiq, accompanied Bahá'u'lláh from 'Iráq to Constantinople, and from there to Adrianople, where he lived happily for some time, close to his Lord. He was humble, long-suffering, thankful; there was always a smile on his lips; he was light of heart, and his soul was in love with Bahá'u'lláh. Later he was given leave to return to 'Iráq, for his family was there, and he remained in that city for a while, dreaming and remembering.

Then a great calamity occurred in 'Iráq, and all four brothers with their noble uncle were taken prisoner. Victimized, captive, they were brought to Mosul. The uncle, Áqá Muḥammad-Riḍá, was an old man, illumined of mind, spiritual of heart, a man detached from all worldly things. He had been extremely rich in 'Iráq, enjoying comforts and pleasures, but now in Hadbá—Mosul—he became the chief victim among the prisoners, and suffered dire need. He was destitute, but remained dignified, patient, content, and thankful. Keeping to himself in an out-of-the-way place, he praised God day and night until he

[1] Qur'án 24:35.

died. He gave up his heart to his heart's Love, burst from the shackles of this inconstant world and ascended to the Kingdom that endures forever. May God immerse him in the waters of forgiveness, make him to enter the garden of His compassion and good pleasure, and keep him in Paradise till the end of time.

As for Muḥammad-Ṣádiq, he too, in Mosul, was subjected to hardships on God's path. He too was a soul at rest, well-pleased with his Lord and well-pleasing unto Him. In the end he too replied to the voice of the King of Glory: "Lord, here am I!" and came to fulfill the verses: "O thou soul which art at rest, return unto thy Lord, well-pleased, and well-pleasing unto Him. Enter thou among My servants; enter Thou My Paradise." [2]

And Muḥammad-'Alí, once he was freed from captivity, hastened from Mosul to the Holy Land, to the precincts of inexhaustible grace. Here he still lives. Although he suffers hardship, his heart is at peace. As for his brother Ibráhím, referred to above, he also came on from Mosul to 'Akká, but to a region close by. There with patience, calm, contentment, but difficulty, he engaged in trade, meanwhile mourning the ascension of Bahá'u'lláh by day and night. Lowly and contrite, with his face turned toward the mysterious realms of God, he wore his life away. At the end, consumed by the years, hardly able to move about, he came to Haifa, where he found a corner of the travelers' hospice to live in, and spent his time humbly calling upon God, entreating Him, offering praise. Little by little, eaten away with age, his person began its dissolution, and at the end he stripped off the garment of flesh and with his unclothed spirit took flight to the realm of the All-Merciful. He was transported out of this dark life into the shining air, and was plunged in a sea of lights. May God brighten his grave

[2] Qur'án 89:27-30.

with spreading rays, and lull his spirit with the fannings of Divine compassion. Upon him be the mercy of God, and His good pleasure.

As for Áqá Ḥabíbu'lláh, he too was made a captive in 'Iráq and was banished away to Mosul. For a long time, he lived in that city, subjected to hardships, but remaining content, and his faith increasing day by day. When famine came to Mosul life was harder than ever on the outsiders, but in the remembrance of God their hearts were at rest,[3] and their souls ate of food from Heaven. Thus they endured it all with astonishing patience, and the people wondered at those strangers in their midst who were neither distressed nor terrified as the others were, and who continued to offer praise day and night. "What amazing trust," the people said, "they have in God!"

Ḥabíb was a man with a great store of patience and a joyous heart. He accustomed himself to exile and he lived in a state of yearning love. After the departure from Baghdád, the prisoners of Mosul were constantly made mention of by Bahá'u'lláh; with regard to them, He expressed His infinite favor. A few years afterward, Ḥabíb hastened away to the encompassing mercy of God, and found a nest and refuge on the boughs of the celestial Tree. There, in the Paradise of all delights, with wondrous songs he poured out his praise of the bountiful Lord.

[3] Cf. Qur'án 13:28: "Truly in the remembrance of God are the hearts set at rest."

Áqá Muḥammad-Ibráhím

MUḤAMMAD-IBRÁHÍM, who bore the title of Manṣúr—Victorious—was a coppersmith. This man of God, yet another among the emigrants and settlers, was a native of Ká<u>sh</u>án. In the early flowering of his youth he recognized the newborn Light and drank deep of the holy cup that is "tempered at the camphor fountain." [1] He was a man of pleasing disposition, full of zest and the joy of life. As soon as the light of faith was lit in his heart, he left Ká<u>sh</u>án, journeyed to Ba<u>gh</u>dád, and was honored with coming into the presence of Bahá'u'lláh.

Áqá Muḥammad had a fine poetic gift, and he would create verses like stringed pearls. In Zawrá—that is, Ba<u>gh</u>dád, the Abode of Peace—he was on amicable terms with friend and stranger alike, ever striving to show forth loving-kindness to all. He brought his brothers from Persia to Ba<u>gh</u>dád, and opened a shop for arts and crafts, applying himself to the welfare of others. He, too, was taken prisoner and exiled from Ba<u>gh</u>dád to Mosul, after which he journeyed to Haifa, where day and night, lowly and humble, he chanted prayers and supplications and centered his thoughts on God.

[1] Qur'án 76:5.

He remained a long time in Haifa, successfully serving the believers there, and most humbly and unobtrusively seeing to the travelers' needs. He married in that city, and fathered fine children. To him every day was a new life and a new joy, and whatever money he made he spent on strangers and friends. After the slaying of the King of Martyrs, he wrote an elegy to memorialize that believer who had fallen on the field of anguish, and recited his ode in the presence of Bahá'u'lláh; the lines were touching in the extreme, so that all who were there shed tears, and voices were raised in grief.

Áqá Muḥammad continued to live out his life, high of aim, unvarying as to his inner condition, with fervor and love. Then he welcomed death, laughing like a rose suddenly full-blown, and crying, "Here am I!" Thus he quitted Haifa, exchanging it for the world above. From this narrow slip of land he hastened upward to the Well-Beloved, soared out of this dust heap to pitch his tent in a fair and shining place. Blessings be unto him, and a goodly home.[2] May God sheathe him in mercies; may he rest under the tabernacles of forgiveness and be brought into the gardens of Heaven.

[2] Qur'án 13:28.

Zaynu'l-'Ábidín Yazdí

One of the emigrants who died along the way to the Holy Land was Zaynu'l-'Ábidín of Yazd. When, in Man<u>sh</u>ád, this devoted man first heard the cry of God, he was awakened to restless life. A holy passion stirred him, his soul was made new. The light of guidance flamed from the lamp of his heart; the love of God sparked a revolution in the country of his inner self. Carried away by love for the Loved One's beauty, he left the home that was dear to him and set out for the Desired Land.

As he traveled along with his two sons, gladdened by hopes of the meeting that would be his, he paused on every hilltop, in every plain, village and hamlet to visit with the friends. But the great distance stretching out before him changed to a sea of troubles, and although his spirit yearned, his body weakened, and at the end he sickened and turned helpless; all this when he was without a home.

Sick as he was, he did not renounce the journey, nor fail in his resolve; he had amazing strength of will, and was determined to keep on; but the illness worsened with every passing day, until at last he winged his way to the mercy of God, and yielded up his soul in a longing unfulfilled.

Although to outward eyes he never drained the cup of meeting, never gazed upon the beauty of Bahá'u'lláh, still he achieved the very spirit of spiritual communion; he is accounted as one of those who attained the Presence, and for him the reward of those who reached that Presence is fixed and ordained. He was a stainless soul, faithful, devoted and true. He never drew a breath except in righteousness, and his single desire was to worship his Lord. He walked the ways of love; he was known to all for steadfast loyalty and pure intent. May God fill up reunion's cup for him in a fair country, make him to enter the everlasting Kingdom, and console his eyes with beholding the lights of that mysterious Realm.

Ḥájí Mullá Mihdíy-i-Yazdí

Yet another who left his homeland was Mullá Mihdí of Yazd. Although to all appearances this excellent man was not of the learned class, he was an expert in the field of Muslim sacred traditions and an eloquent interpreter of orally transmitted texts. Persevering in his devotions, known for holy practices and nightly communings and vigils, his heart was illumined, and he was spiritual of mind and soul. He spent most of his time repeating communes, performing the obligatory prayers, confessing his failings and supplicating the Lord. He was one of those who penetrate mysteries, and was a confidant of the righteous. As a teacher of the Faith he was never at a loss for words, forgetting, as he taught, all restraint, pouring forth one upon another sacred traditions and texts.

When news of him spread around the town and he was everywhere charged, by prince and pauper alike, with bearing this new name, he freely declared his adherence and on this account was publicly disgraced. Then the evil ‘ulamás of Yazd rose up, issuing a decree that he must die. Since the mujtahid, Mullá Báqir of Ardikán, refused to confirm the sentence of those dark divines, Mullá Mihdí lived on, but was forced to leave his native home. With his two sons, one the great martyr-to-be, Jináb-i-Varqá, and the other Jináb-i-Ḥusayn, he set out for the country of his Well-Beloved. In every town and village along the way, he ably spread the Faith, adducing clear arguments and proofs, quoting from and interpreting the sacred traditions and evident signs.[1] He did not rest for a moment; everywhere he shed abroad the attar of the love of God, and diffused the sweet breathings of holiness. And he inspired the friends, making them eager to teach others in their turn, and to excel in knowledge.

He was an eminent soul, with his heart fixed on the beauty of God. From the day he was first created and came into this world, he single-mindedly devoted all his efforts to acquiring grace for the day he should be born into the next.[2] His heart was illumined, his mind spiritual, his soul aspiring, his destination Heaven. He was imprisoned along his way; and as he crossed the deserts and climbed and descended the mountain slopes he endured terrible, uncounted hardships. But the light of faith shone from his brow and in his breast the longing was aflame, and thus he joyously, gladly passed over the frontiers until at last he came to Beirut. In that city, ill, restive, his patience gone, he spent

[1] Qur’án 3:91.
[2] Qur’án 29:19; 53:48; 56:62.

some days. His yearning grew, and his agitation was such that weak and sick as he was, he could wait no more.

He set out on foot for the house of Bahá'u'lláh. Because he lacked proper shoes for the journey, his feet were bruised and torn; his sickness worsened; he could hardly move, but still he went on; somehow he reached the village of Mazra'ih and here, close by the Mansion, he died. His heart found his Well-Beloved One, when he could bear the separation no more. Let lovers be warned by his story; let them know how he gambled away his life in his yearning after the Light of the World. May God give him to drink of a brimming cup in the everlasting gardens; in the Supreme Assemblage, may God shed upon his face rays of light. Upon him be the glory of the Lord. His sanctified tomb is in Mazra'ih, beside 'Akká.

His Eminence Kalím (Mírzá Músá)

Jináb-i-Mírzá Músá was the true brother of Bahá'u'lláh, and from earliest childhood he was reared in the sheltering embrace of the Most Great Name. He drank in the love of God with his mother's milk; when yet a suckling, he showed an extraordinary attachment to the Blessed Beauty. At all times he was the object of Divine grace, favor and loving-kindness. After their distinguished father died, Mírzá Músá was brought up by Bahá'u'lláh, growing to maturity in the haven of His care. Day by day, the youth's servitude and devotion increased. In all things, he lived according to the commandments, and he was entirely severed from any thoughts of this world.

Like a bright lamp, he shone out in that Household. He wished neither rank nor office, and had no worldly aims at all. His one supreme desire was to serve Bahá'u'lláh, and for this reason he was never separated from his Brother's presence. No matter what torments the others inflicted, his loyalty equaled the cruelty of the rest, for he had drunk the wine of unadulterated love.

Then the voice was heard, crying out of Shíráz, and from a single utterance of Bahá'u'lláh's his heart was filled with light, and from a single gust that blew over the gardens of faith, he caught the fragrance. At once, he began to serve the friends. He had an extraordinary attachment to me, and was at all times concerned for my well-being. In Ṭihrán he occupied himself day and night with propagating the Faith and gradually became well known to everyone; habitually he spent his time in the company of blessed souls.

Bahá'u'lláh then left Ṭihrán, journeying to 'Iráq, and of His brothers the two who were in His company were Áqáy-i-Kalím [1] and Mírzá Muḥammad-Qulí. They turned their faces away from Persia and the Persians, and closed their eyes to comfort and peace; in the Beloved's path they chose with all their hearts to bear whatever calamity should be their lot.

Thus they arrived in 'Iráq. During the days when Bahá'u'lláh had vanished from sight, that is, when He was on the journey to Kurdistán, Áqáy-i-Kalím lived on the edge of an abyss; his life was constantly in danger, and each day that passed was worse than the one before; still, he bore it all,

[1] Mírzá Músá.

and knew no fear. When at last the Blessed Beauty returned out of Kurdistán, Áqáy-i-Kalím resumed his post by the Holy Threshold, rendering every service within his power. For this he became known far and wide. At the time when Bahá'u'lláh left Baghdád for Constantinople, Áqáy-i-Kalím was with Him and continued to serve along the way, as he did on the further journey from Constantinople to Adrianople.

It was during the sojourn in this latter city that he detected from Mírzá Yaḥyá the odor of rebellion. Day and night he tried to make him mend his ways, but all to no avail. On the contrary, it was astonishing how, like a deadly poison, the temptings and satanic suggestions of Siyyid Muḥammad worked on Mírzá Yaḥyá, so that Áqáy-i-Kalím finally abandoned hope. Even then he never ceased trying, thinking that somehow, perhaps, he could still the tempest and rescue Mírzá Yaḥyá from the gulf. His heart was worn away with despair and grief. He tried everything he knew. At last he had to admit the truth of these words of Saná'í:

If to the fool my lore you'd bring,
Or think my secrets can be told
To him who is not wise—
Then to the deaf go harp and sing,
Or stand before the blind and hold
A mirror to his eyes.

When all hope was gone, he ended the relationship, saying: "O my brother, if others are in doubt as to this affair, you and I both know the truth. Have you forgotten the loving-kindness of Bahá'u'lláh, and how He trained us both? What care He took with your lessons and your penmanship; how constantly He saw to your spelling and your composition, and encouraged you to practice the different calligraphic styles; He even guided your copy with His own blessed fingers. Who does not know how He showered favors on you, how He brought you up in the haven of His embrace. Is this your thanks for all His tenderness—that you plot with Siyyid Muḥammad and desert the shelter of Bahá'u'lláh? Is this your loyalty? Is this the right return for all His love?" The words had no effect whatever; on the contrary, with each passing day, Mírzá Yaḥyá disclosed a greater measure of his concealed intent. Then at the end, the final rupture took place.

From Adrianople, Áqáy-i-Kalím went on with the convoy of Bahá'u'lláh, to the fortress of 'Akká. His name was specifically listed in the Sulṭán's decree, and he was condemned to perpetual banishment.[2] He devoted all his time in the Most Great Prison to serving Bahá'u'lláh, and had the honor of being continually in his Brother's presence, also keeping company with the believers; until at last he left this world of dust and hastened to the holy world above, dying with lowliness and contrition, as he supplicated his Lord.

It happened that during the Baghdád period, the well-known Ílkhání, son of Músá Khán-i-Qazvíní, received through Siyyid Javád-i-Ṭabáṭabá'í an audience with Bahá'u'lláh. Siyyid Javád on that occasion made a plea in the Ílkhání's behalf, saying: "This Ílkhání, 'Alí-Qulí Khán, although a sinner and a lifelong creature of his passions, has now repented. He stands before You with regret as to his former ways, and from this day forward he will not so much as draw a breath that might be contrary to Your good pleasure. I beg of You, accept his repentance; make him the object of Your grace and favor."

Bahá'u'lláh replied: "Because he has chosen you as intercessor, I will hide away his sins, and I will take steps to bring him comfort and peace of mind."

[2] Cf. *God Passes By,* p. 186.

The Ílkhání had been a man of unlimited wealth, but he had wasted it all on the desires of the flesh. He was now destitute, to such a point that he did not even dare to step outside his house, because of the creditors waiting there to fall upon him. Bahá'u'lláh directed him to go to 'Umar Páshá, the Governor of Damascus, and obtain from him a letter of recommendation to Constantinople. The Ílkhání complied, and he received every assistance from the Governor of Baghdád. After utter despair, he began to hope again, and left for Constantinople. When he arrived at Díyárbakr [3] he penned a letter on behalf of two Armenian merchants. "These two are about to leave for Baghdád," his letter said. "They have shown me every courtesy, and have also asked me for an introduction. I had no refuge or shelter except Your bounty; thus I beg of You to show them favor." The superscription, that is, the address he had written on the envelope was: "To His Eminence Bahá'u'lláh, Leader of the Bábís." The merchants presented this letter to Bahá'u'lláh at the head of the bridge, and when He inquired about it their reply was: "In Díyárbakr, the Ílkhání gave us particulars as to this Cause." Then they accompanied Him to His house.

When the Blessed Beauty entered the family apartments, Áqáy-i-Kalím was there to meet Him. Bahá'u'lláh cried out, "Kalím, Kalím! The fame of the Cause of God has reached as far as Díyárbakr!" And He was smiling, jubilant.

Mírzá Músá was indeed a true brother to the Blessed Beauty; this is why he remained steadfast, under all conditions, to the very end. Unto him be praise and salutations, and the breath of life, and glory; upon him be mercy and grace.

[3] Some four hundred miles northwest of Baghdád.

Ḥájí Muḥammad K͟hán

Another of those who left their homes and came to settle in the neighborhood of Bahá'u'lláh was Ḥájí Muḥammad K͟hán. This distinguished man, a native of Sístán, was a Balú͟ch. When he was very young, he caught fire and became a mystic—an 'árif, or adept. As a wandering dervish, completely selfless, he went out from his home and, following the dervish rule, traveled about in search of his murs͟hid, his perfect leader. For he yearned, as the Qalandar dervishes would say, to discover that "priest of the Magi," or spiritual guide.

Far and wide, he carried on his search. He would speak to everyone he met. But what he longed for was the sweet scent of the love of God, and this he was unable to detect in anyone, whether Gnostic or philosopher, or member of the S͟hayk͟hí sect. All he could see in the dervishes was their tufted beards, and their palms-up religion of beggary. They were "dervish"—poor in all save God—in name only; all they cared about, it seemed to him, was whatever came to hand. Nor did he find illumination among the Illuminati; he heard nothing from them but idle argument. He observed that their grandiloquence was not eloquence and that their subtleties were but windy figures of speech. Truth was not there; the core of inner meaning was absent. For true philosophy is that which produces rewards of excellence, and among these learned men there was no such fruit to be found; at the peak of their accomplishment, they became the slaves of vice, led an unconcerned life and were given over to personal characteristics that were deserving of blame. To him, of all that constitutes the high, distinguishing quality of humankind, they were devoid.

As for the S̲haykh̲í group, their essence was gone, only the dregs remained; the kernel of them had vanished, leaving the shell behind; most of their dialectics was lumber and superfluities by now.

Thus at the very moment when he heard the call from the Kingdom of God, he shouted, "Yea, verily!" and he was off like the desert wind. He traveled over vast distances, arrived at the Most Great Prison and attained the presence of Bahá'u'lláh. When his eyes fell upon that bright Countenance he was instantly enslaved. He returned to Persia so that he could meet with those people who professed to be following the Path, those friends of other days who were seeking out the Truth, and deal with them as his loyalty and duty required.

Both going and returning, the Ḥájí betook himself to each one of his friends, foregathered with them, and let each one hear the new song from Heaven. He reached his homeland and set his family's affairs in order, providing for all, seeing to the security, happiness and comfort of each one. After that he bade them all goodby. To his relatives, his wife, children, kin, he said: "Do not look for me again; do not wait for my return."

He took up a staff and wandered away; over the mountains he went, across the plains, seeking and finding the mystics, his friends. On his first journey, he went to the late Mírzá Yúsuf K̲h̲án (Mustawfíyu'l-Mamálik), in Ṭihrán. When he had said his say, Yúsuf K̲h̲án expressed a wish, and declared that should it be fulfilled, he would believe; the wish was to be given a son. Should such a bounty become his, Yúsuf Khán would be won over. The Ḥájí reported this to Bahá'u'lláh, and received a firm promise in reply. Accordingly, when the Ḥájí met with Yúsuf Khán on his second journey, he found him with a child in his arms. "Mírzá," the Ḥájí cried, "praise be to God! Your test has demonstrated the Truth. You snared your bird of joy." "Yes," answered Yúsuf Khán, "the proof is clear. I am convinced. This year, when you go to Bahá'u'lláh, say that I implore His grace and favor for this child, so that it may be kept safe in the sheltering care of God."

Ḥájí Muḥammad then went to the blissful future martyr, the King of Martyrs, and asked him to intercede, so that he, the Ḥájí, might be allowed to keep watch at the doorway of Bahá'u'lláh. The King of Martyrs sent in this request by letter, after which Ḥájí Khán duly arrived at the Most Great Prison and made his home in the neighborhood of his loving Friend. He enjoyed this honor for a long time, and later, in the Mazra'ih garden as well, he was very frequently in Bahá'u'lláh's presence. After the Beloved had ascended, Ḥájí Khán remained faithful to the Covenant and Testament, shunning the hypocrites. At last, when this servant was absent on the journeys to Europe and America, the Ḥájí made his way to the travelers' hospice at the Ḥaẓíratu'l-Quds; and here, beside the Shrine of the Báb, he took his flight to the world above.

May God refresh his spirit with the musk-scented air of the Abhá Paradise, and the sweet savors of holiness that blow from the highest Heaven. Unto him be greetings and praise. His bright tomb is in Haifa.

Áqá Muḥammad-Ibráhím Amír

Muḥammad-Ibráhím Amír came from Nayríz. He was a blessed person; he was like a cup filled with the red wine of faith. At the time when he was first made captive by the tender Loved One, he was in the flower of his youth. Then he fell a prey to the oppressors, and following the upheaval in Nayríz and all the suffering, his persecutors laid hold of him. Three farrás͟hes pinned his arms and tied his hands behind him; but the Amír by main strength burst his bonds, snatched a dagger from a farras͟h's belt, saved himself and ran away to 'Iráq. There he engaged in writing down the sacred verses and later won the honor of serving at the Holy Threshold. Constant and steadfast, he remained on duty day and night. During the journey from Bag͟hdád to Constantinople, from there to Adrianople, and from there to the Most Great Prison, he was always at hand to serve. He married the handmaid of God, Ḥabíbih, who also served at the Threshold, and his daughter Badí'ih became the helpmeet of the late Ḥusayn-Áqá Qahvih-c͟hí.

Thus the Amír was steadfast in service throughout his life; but after the ascension of Bahá'u'lláh his health steadily declined, and at last he left this world of dust behind him and hastened away to the unsullied world above.

May God illumine the place where he rests with rays from the all-highest Realm. Unto him be salutations and praise. His bright shrine is in 'Akká.

Mírzá Mihdíy-i-Káshání

THIS HONORED man, Mírzá Mihdí, was from Káshán. In early youth, under his father's tutelage, he had studied sciences and arts, and had become skilled in composing both prose and verse, as well as in producing calligraphy in the style known as shikastih.[1] He was singled out from his fellows, head and shoulders above the rest. When still a child, he learned of the Lord's Advent, caught fire with love, and became one of those who "gave their all to purchase Joseph." He was chief of the yearning seekers, lord of lovers; eloquently, he began to teach the Faith, and to prove the validity of the Manifestation.

He made converts; and because he yearned after God, he became a laughing-stock in Káshán, disparaged by friend and stranger alike, exposed to the taunts of his faithless companions. One of them said: "He has lost his mind." And another: "He is a public disgrace. Fortune has turned

[1] Shikastih—broken—a cursive or half-shorthand script, is thought to have been invented at the close of the seventeenth century, in Hirát.

against him. He is done for." The bullies mocked him, and spared him nothing. When life became untenable, and open war broke out, he left his homeland and journeyed to 'Iráq, the focal center of the new Light, where he gained the presence of all mankind's Beloved.

He spent some time here, in the friends' company, composing verses that sang the praises of Bahá'u'lláh. Later he was given leave to return home, and went back to live for a while in Káshán. But again, he was plagued by yearning love, and could bear the separation no more. He returned, therefore, to Baghdád, bringing with him his respected sister, the third consort.

Here he remained, under the bountiful protection of Bahá'u'lláh, until the convoy left 'Iráq for Constantinople, at which time Mírzá Mihdí was directed to remain behind and guard the Holy House. Restless, consumed with longing, he stayed on. When the friends were banished from Baghdád to Mosul, he was among the prisoners, a victim along with the others. With the greatest hardship, he got to Mosul, and here fresh calamities awaited him; he was ill almost all the time, he was an outcast, and destitute. Still he endured it for a considerable period, was patient, retained his dignity, and continually offered thanks. Finally he could bear the absence of Bahá'u'lláh no longer. He sought permission, was granted leave to come, and set out for the Most Great Prison.

Because the way was long and hard, and he suffered cruelly on the journey, when he finally reached the 'Akká prison he was almost helpless, and worn to the bone. It was during the time when the Blessed Beauty was imprisoned within the citadel, at the center of the barracks. Despite the terrible hardships, Mírzá Mihdí spent some days here, in great joy. To him, the calamities were favors, the tribulations were Divine Providence, the chastisement abounding grace; for he was enduring all this on the pathway of God, and seeking to win His good pleasure. His illness worsened; from day to day he failed; then at the last, under sheltering grace, he took his flight to the inexhaustible mercy of the Lord.

This noble personage had been honored among men, but for God's love he lost both name and fame. He bore manifold misfortunes with never a complaint. He was content with God's decrees, and walked the ways of resignation. The glance of Bahá'u'lláh's favor was upon him; he was close to the Divine Threshold. Thus, from the beginning of his life till the end, he remained in one and the same inner state: immersed in an ocean of submission and consent. "O my Lord, take me, take me!" he would cry, until at last he soared away to the world that no man sees.

May God cause him to inhale the sweet scent of holiness in the highest Paradise, and refresh him with the crystalline wine cup, tempered at the camphor fountain.[2] Unto him be salutations and praise. His fragrant tomb is in 'Akká.

Mishkín-Qalam

AMONG THE exiles, neighbors, and prisoners there was also a second Mír 'Imád,[1] the eminent calligrapher,

[2] Qur'án 76:9.

[1] A famed calligrapher who lived and wrote at the court of Sháh-'Abbás, the Ṣafaví (1557-1628).

Mishkín-Qalam.[2] He wielded a musk-black pen, and his brows shone with faith. He was among the most noted of mystics, and had a witty and subtle mind. The fame of this spiritual wayfarer reached out to every land. He was the leading calligrapher of Persia and well known to all the great; he enjoyed a special position among the court ministers of Ṭihrán, and with them he was solidly established.[3] He was famed throughout Asia Minor; his pen was the wonder of all calligraphers, for he was adept at every calligraphic style. He was, besides, a skilled astronomer.

This highly accomplished man first heard of the Cause of God in Iṣfáhán, and the result was that he set out to find Bahá'u'lláh. He crossed the great distances, measured out the miles, climbing mountains, passing over deserts and over the sea, until at last he came to Adrianople. Here he reached the heights of faith and assurance; here he drank the wine of certitude. He responded to the summons of God, he attained the presence of Bahá'u'lláh, he ascended to that apogee where he was received and accepted. By now he was reeling to and fro like a drunkard in his love for God, and because of his violent desire and yearning, his mind seemed to wander. He would be raised up, and then cast down again; he was as one distracted. He spent some time under the sheltering grace of Bahá'u'lláh, and every day new blessings were showered upon him. Meanwhile he produced his splendid calligraphs; he would write out the Most Great Name, Yá Bahá'u'l-Abhá, O Thou Glory of the All-Glorious, with marvelous skill, in many different forms, and would send them everywhere.[4]

[2] Mishk is musk. Mishkín-Qalam means either musk-scented pen, or jet black pen.

[3] Qur'án 61:4.

[4] In some of this artist's productions, the writing was so arranged as to take the forms of birds. When E. G. Browne was in Persia, he was

He was then directed to go on a journey to Constantinople, and set out with Jináb-i-Sayyáḥ. When he reached that Great City, the leading Persians and Turks received him with every honor at first, and they were captivated by his jet black, calligraphic art. He, however, began boldly and eloquently to teach the Faith. The Persian ambassador lurked in ambush; betaking himself to the Sulṭán's vazírs he slandered Mis͟hkín-Qalam. "This man is an agitator," the ambassador told them, "sent here by Bahá'u'lláh to stir up trouble and make mischief in this Great City. He has already won over a large company, and he intends to subdue still more. These Bahá'ís turned Persia upside down; now they have started in on the capital of Turkey. The Persian Government put 20,000 of them to the sword, hoping by this tactic to quench the fires of sedition. You should awaken to the danger; soon this perverse thing will blaze up here as well. It will consume the harvest of your life; it will burn up the whole world. Then you can do nothing, for it will be too late."

Actually that mild and submissive man, in that throne city of Asia Minor, was occupied solely with his calligraphy and his worship of God. He was striving to bring about not sedition but fellowship and peace. He was seeking to reconcile the followers of different faiths, not to drive them

---

told that "these would be eagerly sought after by Persians of all classes, were it not that they all bore, as the signature of the penman, the following verse:

Dar díyár-i-k͟haṭṭ s͟háh-i-ṣáḥib-'alam
Bandiy-i-báb-i-Bahá, Mis͟hkín-Qalam."

Cf. *A Year Amongst the Persians,* p. 227. The verse might be translated:

Lord of calligraphy, my banner goes before;
But to Bahá'u'lláh, a bondsman at the door,
Naught else I am,
Mis͟hkín-Qalam.

Note the wordplay on door, which makes possible the inclusion of the Báb's name as well as Bahá'u'lláh's.

still further apart. He was of service to strangers and was helping to educate the native people. He was a refuge to the hapless and a horn of plenty to the poor. He invited all comers to the oneness of humankind; he shunned hostility and malice.

The Persian ambassador, however, wielded enormous power, and he had maintained close ties with the ministers for a very long time. He prevailed on a number of persons to insinuate themselves into various gatherings and there to make every kind of false charge against the believers. Urged on by the oppressors, spies began to surround Mishkín-Qalam. Then, as instructed by the ambassador, they carried reports to the Prime Minister, stating that the individual in question was stirring up mischief day and night, that he was a trouble maker, a rebel and a criminal. The result was, they jailed him and they sent him away to Gallipoli, where he joined our own company of victims. They despatched him to Cyprus and ourselves to the 'Akká prison. On the island of Cyprus, Jináb-i-Mishkín was held prisoner in the citadel at Famagusta, and in this city he remained, a captive, from the year 85 till 94.

When Cyprus passed out of Turkish hands, Mishkín-Qalam was freed and betook himself to his Well-Beloved in the city of 'Akká, and here he lived encompassed by the grace of Bahá'u'lláh, producing his marvelous calligraphs and sending them about. He was at all times joyous of spirit, ashine with the love of God, like a candle burning its life away, and he was a consolation to all the believers.

After the ascension of Bahá'u'lláh, Mishkín-Qalam remained loyal, solidly established in the Covenant. He stood before the violators like a brandished sword. He would never go half way with them; he feared no one but God; not for a moment did he falter, nor ever fail in service.

Following the ascension he made a journey to India,

where he associated with the lovers of truth. He spent some time there, making fresh efforts every day. When I learned that he was getting helpless, I sent for him at once and he came back to this Most Great Prison, to the joy of the believers, who felt blessed to have him here again. He was at all times my close companion. He had amazing verve, intense love. He was a compendium of perfections: believing, confident, serene, detached from the world, a peerless companion, a wit—and his character like a garden in full bloom. For the love of God, he left all good things behind; he closed his eyes to success, he wanted neither comfort nor rest, he sought no wealth, he wished only to be free from the defilement of the world. He had no ties to this life, but spent his days and nights supplicating and communing with God. He was always smiling, effervescing; he was spirit personified, love embodied. For sincerity and loyalty he had no match, nor for patience and inner calm. He was selflessness itself, living on the breaths of the spirit.

If he had not been in love with the Blessed Beauty, if he had not set his heart on the Realm of Glory, every worldly pleasure could have been his. Wherever he went, his many calligraphic styles were a substantial capital, and his great accomplishment brought him attention and respect from rich and poor alike. But he was hopelessly enamored of man's one true Love, and thus he was free of all those other bonds, and could float and soar in the spirit's endless sky.

Finally, when I was absent, he left this darksome, narrow world and hastened away to the land of lights. There, in the haven of God's boundless mercy, he found infinite rewards. Unto him be praise and salutations, and the Supreme Companion's tender grace.

Ustád 'Alí-Akbar-i-Najjár

USTÁD 'ALÍ-AKBAR, the Cabinet-Maker,[1] was numbered among the just, a prince of the righteous. He was one of Persia's earliest believers and a leading member of that company. From the beginning of the Cause a trusted confidant, he loosed his tongue to proclaim the Faith. He informed himself as to its proofs, and went deep into its Scriptures. He was also a gifted poet, writing odes in eulogy of Bahá'u'lláh.

Exceptionally skilled in his craft, Ustád produced highly ingenious work, fashioning carpentry that, for intricacy and precision, resembled mosaic inlay. He was expert in mathematics as well, solving and explaining difficult problems.

From Yazd, this revered man traveled to 'Iráq, where he achieved the honor of entering the presence of Bahá'u'lláh, and received abundant grace. The Blessed Beauty showered favors upon Ustád 'Alí, who entered His presence almost every day. He was one of those who were exiled from Baghdád to Mosul, and he endured severe hardships there. He remained a long time in Mosul, in extremely straitened

[1] Ustád is a master, one who is skilled in an art or profession.

circumstances but resigned to the will of God, always in prayer and supplication, and with a thankful tongue.

Finally he came from Mosul to the Holy Shrine and here by the tomb of Bahá'u'lláh he would meditate and pray. In the dark of the night, restless and uneasy, he would lament and cry out; when he was supplicating God his heart burned within him; his eyes would shed their tears, and he would lift up his voice and chant. He was completely cut off from this dust heap, this mortal world. He shunned it, he asked but one thing—to soar away; and he hoped for the promised recompense to come. He could not bear for the Light of the World to have disappeared, and what he sought was the paradise of reunion with Him, and what his eyes hungered to behold was the glory of the Abhá Realm. At last his prayer was answered and he rose upward into the world of God, to the gathering-place of the splendors of the Lord of Lords.

Upon him be God's benediction and praise, and may God bring him into the abode of peace, as He has written in His book: "For them is an abode of peace with their Lord." [2] "And to those who serve Him, is God full of kindness." [3]

[2] Qur'án 6:127.
[3] Qur'án 3:28.

S͟hayk͟h 'Alí-Akbar-i-Mázgání

THIS CHIEF of free souls, of wanderers for the love of God, was only an infant when, in Mázgán, he was suckled at the breast of grace. He was a child of the eminent scholar, S͟hayk͟h-i-Mázgání; his noble father was one of the leading citizens of Qamṣar, near Kás͟hán, and for piety, holiness, and the fear of God he had no peer. This father embodied all the qualities that are worthy of praise; moreover his ways were pleasing, his disposition good, he was an excellent companion, and for all these things he was well known. When he threw off restraint and openly declared himself a believer, the faithless, whether friend or stranger, turned their backs on him and began to plot his death. But he continued to further the Cause, to alert the people's hearts, and to welcome the newcomers as generously as ever. Thus in Kás͟hán the fame of his strong faith reached as high as the Milky Way. Then the pitiless aggressors rose up, plundered his possessions and killed him.

'Alí-Akbar, the son of him who had laid down his life in the pathway of God, could live in that place no longer. Had he remained, he too, like his father, would have been put to the sword. He passed some time in 'Iráq, and received the honor of being in the presence of Bahá'u'lláh. Then he went back to Persia, but again he longed to look upon Bahá'u'lláh, and with his wife he set out over the deserts and mountains, sometimes riding, sometimes on foot, measuring off the miles, passing from one shore to the other, reaching the Holy Place at last and in the shade of the Divine Lote-Tree finding safety and peace.

When the beauty of the Desired One had vanished from this world, 'Alí-Akbar remained loyal to the Covenant and prospered under the grace of God. By disposition and because of the intense love in his heart, he yearned to write poetry, to fashion odes and ghazals, but he lacked both meter and rhyme:

I planned a poem, but my Beloved told me,
"Plan only this, that thine eyes should behold Me."

With rapturous longing, his heart desired the realms of his compassionate Lord; consumed by burning love, he left this world at last, and pitched his tent in the world above. May God send down upon his grave, from the Kingdom of His forgiveness, a heavy rain [1] of blessings, bestow a great victory upon him, and grant him mercies, pressed down and running over, in the retreats of Heaven.

[1] Qur'án 2:266, 267.

Mírzá Muḥammad, the Servant at the Travelers' Hospice

THIS YOUTH of God was from Iṣfáhán, and from an early age was known to its leading divines for his excellent mind. He was of gentle birth, his family was known and respected, and he was an accomplished scholar. He had profited from philosophy and history alike, from sciences and arts, but he thirsted after the secret of reality, and longed for knowledge of God. His feverish thirst was not allayed by the arts and sciences, however limpid those waters. He kept on seeking, seeking, carrying on debates in gatherings of learned men until at last he discovered the meaning of his longing dream, and the enigma, the inviolable secret, lay open before him. Suddenly he caught the scent of fresh flowers from the gardens of the splendor of God, and his heart was ashine with a ray from the Sun of Truth. Whereas before, he was like a fish taken from the water, now he had come to the wellspring of eternal life; before, he was a questing moth; now he had found the candle flame. A true seeker after truth, he was instantly revived by the supreme Glad Tidings; his heart's eye was brightened by the new dawn of guidance. So blinding was the fire of Divine love that he turned his face away from his life, its peace, its blessings, and set out for the Most Great Prison.

In Iṣfáhán he had enjoyed every comfort, and the world was good to him. Now his yearning for Bahá'u'lláh freed him from all other bonds. He passed over the long miles, suffered intense hardships, exchanged a palace for a prison, and in the 'Akká fortress assisted the believers and attended upon and served Bahá'u'lláh. He who had been waited upon, now waited on others; he who had been the master was now the servant, he who had once been a leader was now a captive. He had no rest, no leisure, day or night. To the travelers he was a trusted refuge; to the settlers, a companion without peer. He served beyond his strength, for he was filled with love of the friends. The travelers were devoted to him, and the settlers grateful. And because he was continuously busy, he kept silent at all times.

Then the Supreme Affliction came upon us and the absence of Bahá'u'lláh was not to be endured. Mírzá Muḥammad could not stay quiet, day or night. He wasted away, like a candle burning down; from the fiery anguish, his liver and heart were inflamed, and his body could bear no more. He wept and supplicated day and night, yearning to soar away to that undiscovered country. "Lord, free me, free me from this absence," he would cry, "let me drink of reunion's cup, find me a lodging in the shelter of Thy mercy, Lord of Lords!"

At last he quit this dust heap, the earth, and took his flight to the world that has no end. May it do him good, that cup brimming with the grace of God, may he eat with healthy relish of that food which gives life to heart and soul. May God lead him to that happy journey's end and grant him an abundant share in the gifts which shall then be bestowed.[1]

[1] For some of these Arabic phrases, see Qur'án 3:170; 4:12, 175; 5:16, 17; 11:100, 101; 28:79; 41:35.

Mírzá Muḥammad-i-Vakíl

One of the captives who were sent on from Baghdád to Mosul was Mírzá Muḥammad-i-Vakíl. This righteous soul was among those who became believers in Baghdád. It was there he drank from the cup of resignation to the will of God and sought his rest in the shade of the celestial Tree. He was a man high-minded and worthy of trust. He was also an extremely capable and energetic administrator of important affairs, famous in 'Iráq for his wise counsel. After he became a believer, he was distinguished by the title of Vakíl—deputy. It happened in this way:

There was a notable in Baghdád by the name of Ḥájí Mírzá Hádí, the jeweler. He had a distinguished son, Áqá Mírzá Músá, who had received from Bahá'u'lláh the title "Letter of Eternity." This son had become a staunch believer. As for his father, the Ḥájí, he was a princely individual known for his lavish open-handedness not only in Persia and 'Iráq but as far away as India. To begin with he had been a Persian vazír; but when he saw how the late Fatḥ-'Alí Sháh eyed worldly riches, particularly the worldly riches of Persian vazírs, and how he snatched whatever they had accumulated, and how, not content with confiscating their costly vanities and lumber, he punished and tortured them right and left, calling it a legal penalty—the Ḥájí dreaded that he too might be catapulted into the abyss. He abandoned his position as vazír, and his mansion, and fled to Baghdád. Fatḥ-'Alí Sháh demanded that the Governor of Baghdád, Dávúd Páshá, send him back, but the Páshá was a man of courage and the Ḥájí was widely known for his able mind. Accordingly, the Páshá respected and helped him and the Ḥájí set up in business as a jeweler. He lived with pomp and splendor, like a great prince. He was one of the most remarkable men of his time, for within his palace he carried on a life of gratification and opulence, but he left his pomp, style and retinue behind, occupied himself with his business affairs and realized great profits.

The door of his house was always open. Turks and Persians, neighbors, strangers from far places, all were his honored guests. Most of Persia's great, when they came on pilgrimage to the Holy Shrines, would stop at his house, where they would find a banquet laid out, and every luxury ready to hand. The Ḥájí was, indeed, more distinguished than Persia's Grand Vazír; he outshone all the vazírs for magnificence, and as the days passed by he dispensed ever more largesse to all who came and went. He was the pride of the Persians throughout 'Iráq, the glory of his fellow nationals. Even on the Turkish vazírs and ministers and the grandees of Baghdád he bestowed gifts and favors; and for intelligence and perceptivity he had no equal.

Because of the Ḥájí's advancing years, toward the end of his days his business affairs declined. Still, he made no change in his way of life. Exactly as before, he continued to live with elegance. The prominent would borrow heavily from him, and never pay him back. One of them, the mother of Áqá Khán Maḥallátí, borrowed 100,000 túmáns[1] from him and did not repay one penny, for she died soon after. The Íl-Khán, 'Alí-Qulí Khán, was another debtor; another was Sayfu'd-Dawlih, a son of Fatḥ-'Alí Sháh; another, Válíyyih, a daughter of Fatḥ-'Alí Sháh; these are only a few examples out of many, from among the Turkish amírs and the great of Persia and 'Iráq. All these debts remained unpaid and irrecoverable. Nevertheless, that eminent and princely man continued to live exactly as before.

Toward the close of his life he conceived a remarkable love for Bahá'u'lláh, and most humbly, would enter His presence. I remember him saying one day, to the Blessed Beauty, that in the year 1250 and something over, Mírzá Mawkab the famed astrologer visited the Shrines. "One day he said to me," the Ḥají continued, " 'Mírzá, I see a strange, a unique conjunction in the stars. It has never occurred before. It proves that a momentous event is about to take place, and I am certain that this event can be nothing less than the Advent of the promised Qá'im.' "

Such was the situation of that illustrious prince when he passed away, leaving as heirs a son and two daughters. Thinking him to be as wealthy as ever, the people believed that his heirs would inherit millions, for everyone knew his way of life. The Persian diplomatic representative, the latter-day mujtahids, and the faithless judge all sharpened their teeth. They started a quarrel among the heirs, so that in the resulting turmoil they themselves would make substantial gains. With this in view they did whatever they could to ruin the heirs, the idea being to strip the inheritors bare, while the Persian diplomat, the mujtahids, and the judge would accumulate the spoils.

Mírzá Músá was a staunch believer; his sisters, how-

[1] The Baghdád period in Bahá'í history was from April 8, 1853 to May 3, 1863. According to various estimates the túmán of the day ranged from $1.08 to $1.60.

ever, were from a different mother, and they knew nothing of the Cause. One day the two sisters, accompanied by the son-in-law of the late Mírzá Siyyid Riḍá, came to the house of Bahá'u'lláh. The two sisters entered the family apartments while the son-in-law settled down in the public reception rooms. The two girls then said to Bahá'u'lláh: "The Persian envoy, the judge, and the faithless mujtahids have destroyed us. Toward the close of his life, the late Ḥájí trusted no one but Yourself. We ourselves have been remiss and we should have sought Your protection before; in any case we come now to implore Your pardon and help. Our hope is that You will not send us away despairing, and that through Your favor and support we shall be saved. Deign, then, to look into this affair, and to overlook our past mistakes."

Replying, the Blessed Beauty declared with finality that intervention in affairs of this kind was abhorrent to Him. They kept on pleading with Him, however. They remained a whole week in the family apartments, clamoring every morning and evening for favor and grace. "We will not lift our heads from off this Threshold," they said. "We will seek sanctuary here in this house; we will remain here, by the door of Him Who guards the angels, until He shall deign to look into our concerns and to save us from our oppressors."

Each day, Bahá'u'lláh would counsel them, saying, "Matters of this kind are in the hands of the mujtahids and the government authorities. We do not interfere in such affairs." But they kept on with their importunities, insisting, imploring, begging for help. It happened that the house of Bahá'u'lláh was bare of worldly goods, and these ladies, accustomed to the best of everything, could hardly be satisfied with bread and water. Food had to be procured for them on credit. Briefly, from every direction, there were problems.

Finally one day Bahá'u'lláh summoned me to His presence. "These esteemed ladies," He said, "with all their exactions, have put Us to considerable inconvenience. There is no help for it—you will have to see to this case. But you must solve this entire, complicated matter in a single day."

The next morning, accompanied by Áqáy-i-Kalím, I went to the house of the late Ḥájí. We called in appraisers and they collected all the jewels in an upper apartment; the ledgers and account books having to do with the properties were placed in a second room; the costly furnishings and art objects of the house in a third. A number of jewelers then went to work and set a value on the gems. Other experts appraised the house, the shops, the gardens, the baths. As soon as they began their work I came out and posted someone in each room so that the appraisers could duly complete their tasks. By this time it was nearly noon. We then had luncheon, after which the appraisers were directed to divide everything into two equal parts, so that lots could be cast; one part would be that of the daughters, and one that of the son, Mírzá Músá.[2] I then went to bed, for I was ill. In the afternoon I rose, had tea, and repaired to the family apartments of the mansion. Here I observed that the goods had been divided into three parts. I said to them: "My instructions were that everything should be divided into two parts. How is it that there are three?" The heirs and other relatives answered as one: "A third must certainly be set aside. That is why we have divided everything into three. One share is for Mírzá Músá, one for the two daughters, and the third we place at Your disposal; this third is the portion of the deceased and You are to expend it in any way You see fit."

Greatly disturbed, we told them, "Such a thing is out of the question. This you must not require, for it cannot

[2] This was in accord with the law of Islám. Cf. Qur'án 4:12.

be complied with. We gave our word to Bahá'u'lláh that not so much as a copper coin would be accepted." But they, too, swore upon oath that it must be as they wished, that they would agree to nothing else. This servant answered: "Let us leave this matter for the present. Is there any further disagreement among you?" "Yes," said Mírzá Músá, "what has become of the money that was left?" Asked the amount, he answered: "Three hundred thousand túmáns." The daughters said: "There are two possibilities: either this money is here in the house, in some coffer, or buried hereabouts—or else it is in other hands. We will give over the house and all its contents to Mírzá Músá. We two will leave the house, with nothing but our veils. If anything turns up we, as of now, freely accord it to him. If the money is elsewhere, it has no doubt been deposited in someone's care; and that person, well aware of the breach of trust, will hardly come forward, deal honorably by us, and return it—rather, he will make off with it all. Mírzá Músá must establish a satisfactory proof of what he says; his claim alone is not evidence." Mírzá Músá replied: "All the property was in their hands; I knew nothing of what was going on—I had no hint of it. They did whatever they pleased."

In short, Mírzá Músá had no clear proof of his claim. He could only ask, "Is such a thing possible, that the late Ḥájí had no ready funds?" Since the claim was unsupported, I felt that pursuing it further would lead to a scandal and produce nothing of value. Accordingly I bade them: "Cast the lots." As for the third share, I had them put it in a separate apartment, close it off, and affix a seal to the door. The key I brought to Bahá'u'lláh. "The task is done," I said. "It was accomplished only through Your confirmations. Otherwise it could not have been completed in a year. However, a difficulty has arisen." I described in detail the claim of Mírzá Músá and the absence of any proof. Then I said, "Mírzá Músá is heavily in debt. Even should he expend all he has, still he could not pay off his creditors. It is best, therefore, if You Yourself will accept the heirs' request, since they persist in their offer, and bestow that share on Mírzá Músá. Then he could at least free himself from his debts and still have something left over."

On the following day the heirs appeared and implored the Blessed Beauty to have me accept the third share. "This is out of the question," He told them. Then they begged and entreated Him to accept that share Himself and expend it for charitable purposes of His own choice. He answered: "There is only one purpose for which I might expend that sum." They said, "That is no concern of ours, even if You have it thrown into the sea. We will not loose our hold from the hem of Your garment and we will not cease our importunities until You accede to our request." Then He told them, "I have now accepted this third share; and I have given it to Mírzá Músá, your brother, but on the condition that, from this day forward, he will speak no more of any claim against yourselves." The heirs were profuse in their thanks. And so this weighty and difficult case was settled in a single day. It left no residue of complaints, no uproar, no further quarrels.

Mírzá Músá did his best to urge some of the jewels on me, but I refused. Finally he requested that I accept a single ring. It was a precious ring, set with a costly pomegranate ruby, a flawless sphere, and unique. All around the central stone, it was gemmed with diamonds. This too I refused, although I had no 'abá to my back and nothing to wear but a cotton tunic that bespoke the antiquity of the world, nor did I own a copper coin. As Ḥáfiẓ would say: "An empty purse, but in our sleeve a hoard."

Grateful for the bounty he had received, Mírzá Músá

offered Bahá'u'lláh everything he possessed: orchards, lands, estates—but it was refused. Then he appointed the 'ulamás of 'Iráq to intercede for him. They hastened to Bahá'u'lláh in a body and begged Him to accept the proffered gifts. He categorically refused. They respectfully told Him: "Unless You accept, in a very short time Mírzá Músá will scatter it all to the winds. For his own good, he should not have access to this wealth."

Then in his own hand, Mírzá Músá penned deeds of gift, made out according to each of the five creeds, in Arabic and Persian; two copies he made, and chose the 'ulamás as his witnesses. Through certain 'ulamás of Baghdád, among them the famed scholar 'Abdu's-Salám Effendi, and the erudite and widely known Siyyid Dávúd Effendi, he presented the deed of gift to Bahá'u'lláh. The Blessed Beauty told them: "We are appointing Mírzá Músá himself as Our deputy."

After Bahá'u'lláh's departure for Rumelia, Mírzá Músá, with a promissory note, purchased from the Government the tithes of Hindíyyih, a district near Karbilá, and suffered a terrible loss, close to 100,000 túmáns. The Government confiscated his properties and sold them for next to nothing. When told of the matter, Bahá'u'lláh said, "Do not speak of this, ever again. Do not so much as utter a word about those estates." Meanwhile the exile from Adrianople to 'Akká took place. Mírzá Muḥammad went to the Government authorities and said to them: "I am the deputy (vakíl) of Bahá'u'lláh. These properties do not belong to Mírzá Músá. How is it that you have taken them over?" But he had no documents to support him, for the title deeds were in 'Akká, and on this account the Government rejected his claim. However, in the process, he became known to all as Mírzá Muḥammad the Deputy. This is how he received the title.

When we were in Adrianople, Mírzá Músá sent on the

ruby ring, through Siyyid 'Alí-Akbar, and the Blessed Beauty directed us to accept it. After we reached 'Akká the believers fell ill, and lay suffering in their beds. I sent the ring to India, to one of the friends, asking him to sell it with all possible speed and forward the proceeds to us in 'Akká to be expended on the sick. That blessed individual never sent us a penny. Two years later he wrote to say that he had sold the ring for twenty-five pounds and had spent that sum on the pilgrims. This, when the ring was of such great value. I made no complaint. Rather, I praised God, thanking Him that out of all that wealth not a fleck of dust had settled on my robe.

Mírzá Muḥammad was taken prisoner and sent away from Baghdád to Mosul, where he fell a prey to fearful ills. He had been rich; in God's path he was now poor. He had enjoyed his ease and comfort; now, for the love of God, he suffered pain and toil. He lived on for a time in Mosul, suppliant, resigned, and lowly. And then, severed from all save God, irresistibly drawn by the gentle gales of the Lord, he rose out of this dark world to the land of light. Unto him be salutations and praise. May God shed down upon him the waters of forgiveness, and open before his grave the gates of Heaven.

Ḥájí Muḥammad-Riḍáy-i-Shírází

Ḥájí Muḥammad-Riḍá came from Shíráz. He was a man spiritually minded, lowly, contrite, the embodiment of serenity and faith. When the call of God was lifted up, that needy soul hurried into the shelter of heavenly grace. As soon as he heard the summons, "Am I not your Lord?" he cried out: "Yea, verily!" [1] and became as a lamp to the people's feet.

For a long time he served the Afnán, Ḥájí Mírzá Muḥammad-'Alí, and was his loyal and close companion, trusted in all things. Later, following a journey to distant countries, he went to the Holy Land, and there in utter submission and lowliness bowed his head before the Sacred Threshold and was honored with entering the presence of Bahá'u'lláh, where he drank in endless bounties from cupped hands. For quite a time he remained there, attending upon Bahá'u'lláh almost every day, encompassed by holy favor and grace. He was outstanding as to character, and lived after the commandments of God: tranquil and long-suffering, in his surrender to God's will he was selflessness itself. He had no personal aims whatever, no feeling of attachment to this fleeting world. His

[1] Qur'án 7:171.

one desire was to please his Lord, his one hope, to walk the holy path.

He went on, then, to Beirut, serving the honored Afnán in that city. He spent a long time in this wise, returning again and again to enter the presence of Bahá'u'lláh and gaze upon that Most Great Beauty. Later, in Sidon, he fell ill. Unable to make the journey to 'Akká, in perfect acquiescence and contentment he ascended to the Abhá Kingdom, and was plunged in the ocean of lights. By the Supreme Pen, endless bounty was bestowed upon his memory. He was indeed one of the loyal, the steadfast, a solid pillar of servitude to Bahá'u'lláh. Many and many a time, from the lips of the Blessed Beauty, we heard his praise.

Unto him be greetings and praise, and the glory of the All-Glorious. Upon him be compassion and most great mercy from the Lord of the High Heavens. His shining grave is in Sidon, near the place called the Station of John the Holy.

Ḥusayn Effendi Tabrízí

THIS YOUTH was from Tabríz, and he was filled with the love of God like a cup flowing and brimming over with red wine. In the flower of his youth he left Persia and traveled to Greece, making his living as a merchant there; till a day came when, guided by Divine bounty, he went from Greece to Smyrna, and there he was given the glad tidings of a new Manifestation on earth. He shouted aloud, was frenzied, was drunk with the music of the new message. He escaped from his debits and credits, set out to meet the Lord of his heart, and entered the presence of Bahá'u'lláh. For some time, a trusted attendant and companion, he served the Blessed Beauty. He was then directed to seek a lodging in the city of Haifa.

Here he faithfully waited upon the believers, and his home was a way station for Bahá'í travelers. He had an excellent disposition, a wonderful character, and high, spiritual aims. He was friendly with friend and stranger alike; he was kind to people of every nation and wished them well.

When the Most Great Light ascended to the Concourse above, Ḥusayn Effendi remained faithful to Him, steadfast and firm; and as before, he continued to be a close friend to the friends. Thus he lived for a considerable period, and felt himself better off than the kings of the earth. He became the son-in-law of Mírzá Muḥammad-Qulí, brother of the Blessed Beauty, and remained for a time peaceful and serene. He carefully avoided any occasion of being seduced into error, for he dreaded that the tempest of afflictions might mount in fury, surge ever higher, and sweep many a soul into the fathomless gulf.[1] He would sigh and mourn, for this fear was with him at all times. At last he could bear the world no longer, and with his own hands stripped off the garment of life.

Praise be unto him, and salutations, and the mercy of God, and Divine acceptance. May God pardon him and make him to enter the highest Heaven, the Paradise that towers above all the rest. His sweet-scented grave is in Haifa.

[1] For the tribulations following Bahá'u'lláh's departure see *God Passes By*, chapter XV.

Jamshíd-i-Gurjí

YET ANOTHER of the emigrants and settlers was the valiant Jamshíd-i-Gurjí, who came from Georgia, but grew up in the city of Káshán. He was a fine youth, faithful, trustworthy, with a high sense of honor. When he heard of a new Faith dawning, and awoke to the tidings that on Persia's horizons the Sun of Truth had risen, he was filled with holy ecstasy, and he longed and loved. The new fire burned away those veils of uncertainty and doubt that had closed him round; the light of Truth shed down its rays, the lamp of guidance burned before him.

He remained in Persia for a time, then left for Rumelia, which was Ottoman territory, and in the Land of Mystery, Adrianople, won the honor of entering the presence of Bahá'u'lláh; it was there that his meeting took place. His joy and fervor were boundless. Later, at Bahá'u'lláh's command he made a journey to Constantinople, with Áqá Muḥammad-Báqir and Áqá 'Abdu'l-Ghaffár. In that city, the tyrannous imprisoned him and put him in chains.

The Persian ambassador informed against Jamshíd and Ustád Muḥammad-'Alí-i-Dallák as enemy leaders and fighters. Jamshíd he described as a latter-day Rustam[1]

[1] Persia's Hercules.

while Muḥammad-'Alí, according to the envoy, was a ravening lion. These two respected men were first imprisoned and caged; then they were sent out of Turkish territory, under guard to the Persian frontier. They were to be delivered over to the Persian Government and crucified, and the guards were threatened with terrible punishments should they once relax their vigilance and let the prisoners escape. For this reason, at every stopping place the victims were kept in some almost inaccessible spot. Once they were thrown into a pit, a kind of well, and suffered agonies all through the night. The next morning Jams͟híd cried out: "O you who oppress us! Are we Joseph the Prophet that you have thrown us in this well? Remember how He rose out of the well as high as the full moon? We too walk the pathway of God, we too are down here for His sake, and we know that these depths are the heights of the Lord."

Once arrived at the Persian frontier, Jams͟híd and Muḥammad-'Alí were handed over to Kurdish chiefs to be sent on to Ṭihrán. The Kurdish chiefs could see that the prisoners were innocent men, kindly and well-disposed, who had fallen a prey to their enemies. Instead of dispatching them to the capital, they set them free. Joyfully, the two hastened away on foot, went back to Bahá'u'lláh and found a home close by Him in the Most Great Prison.

Jams͟híd spent some time in utter bliss, receiving the grace and favor of Bahá'u'lláh and ever and again being admitted to His presence. He was tranquil and at peace. The believers were well-pleased with him, and he was well-pleased with God. It was in this condition that he hearkened to the celestial bidding: "O thou soul which art at rest, return unto thy Lord, well-pleased with Him, and well-pleasing unto Him." [2] And to God's cry: "Return!"

[2] Qur'án 89:27.

he replied, "Yea, verily!" He rose out of the Most Great Prison to the highest Heaven; he soared away to a pure and gleaming Kingdom, out of this world of dust. May God succor him in the celestial company,[3] bring him into the Paradise of Splendors, and safe in the Divine gardens, make him to live forevermore.

Salutations be unto him, and praise. His grave, sweet as musk, is in 'Akká.

Ḥájí Ja'far-i-Tabrízí and His Brothers

THERE WERE three brothers, all from Tabríz: Ḥájí Ḥasan, Ḥájí Ja'far, and Ḥájí Taqí. These three were like eagles soaring; they were three stars of the Faith, pulsing with the light of the love of God.

Ḥájí Ḥasan was of the earlier day; he had believed from the new Luminary's first dawning. He was full of ardor, keen of mind. After his conversion he traveled everywhere, through the cities and villages of Persia, and his breath moved the hearts of longing souls. Then he left for Iráq, and on the Beloved's first journey, attained His presence there. Once he beheld that beauteous Light he was carried away to the Kingdom of Splendors; he was incandescent, he became a thrall of yearning love. At this

[3] Qur'án 4:71.

time he was directed to go back to Persia. He was a peddler, a vendor of small wares, and would travel from city to city.

On Bahá'u'lláh's second journey to 'Iráq, Ḥájí Ḥasan longed to behold Him again, and there in Baghdád was once more bedazzled by His presence. Every so often he would journey to Persia and then return, his thoughts centered on teaching and furthering the Cause. His business fell apart. His merchandise was carried away by thieves, and thus, as he put it, his load was lifted from him—he was disencumbered. He shunned every worldly tie. He was held fast as by a magnet; he fell hopelessly, madly in love with the tender Companion, with Him Who is the Well-Beloved of both worlds. He was known everywhere for the ecstasy he was in, and experienced strange states of being; sometimes, with utmost eloquence, he would teach the Faith, adducing as proofs many a sacred verse and holy tradition, and bringing sound and reasonable arguments to bear. Then his hearers would comment on the power of his mind, on his wisdom and his self-possession. But there were other times when love suddenly flamed within him, and then he could not remain still for an instant. At those times he would skip, and dance, or again in a loud voice he would cry out a verse from the poets, or a song. Toward the end of his days he became a close friend of Jináb-i-Muníb; the two exchanged many a recondite confidence, and each carried many a melody in his breast.

On the friends' final journey he went to Ádhirbáyján, and there, throwing caution to the winds, he roared out the Greatest Name: "Yá Bahá'u'l-Abhá!" The unbelievers there joined forces with his relatives, and they lured that innocent, that man in his ecstasy, away to a garden. Here, they first put questions to him and listened to his answers. He spoke out; he expounded the secret verities of the

Faith, and set forth conclusive proofs that the Advent had indeed come to pass. He recited verses from the Qur'án, and traditions handed down from the Prophet Muḥammad and the Holy Imáms. Following that, in a frenzy of love and longing rapture, he began to sing. It was a s͟hahnáz melody he sang; the words were from the poets, to say that the Lord had come. And they killed him; they shed his blood. They wrenched and hacked his limbs apart and hid his body underneath the dust.

As for Ḥájí Muḥammad-Ja'far, the gently born, he too, like his brother, was bewitched by the Blessed Beauty. It was in 'Iráq that he entered the presence of the Light of the World, and he too caught fire with Divine love and was carried away by the gentle gales of God. Like his brother, he was a vendor of small wares, always on a journey from one place to the next. When Bahá'u'lláh left Bag͟hdád for the capital of Islám, Ḥájí Ja'far was in Persia, and when the Blessed Beauty and His retinue came to a halt in Adrianople, Ja'far and Ḥájí Taqí, his brother, arrived there from Ád͟hirbáyján. They found a corner somewhere and settled down. Our oppressors then stretched out arrogant hands to send Bahá'u'lláh forth to the Most Great Prison, and they forbade the believers to accompany the true Beloved, for it was their purpose to bring the Blessed Beauty to this prison with but a few of His people. When Ḥájí Ja'far saw that they had excluded him from the band of exiles, he seized a razor and slashed his throat.[1] The crowds expressed their grief and horror and the authorities then permitted all the believers to leave in company wth Bahá'u'lláh—this because of the blessing that came from Ja'far's act of love.

They stitched up his wound but no one thought he would recover. They told him, "For the time being, you

[1] Cf. *God Passes By,* p. 180.

will have to stay where you are. If your throat heals, you will be sent on, along with your brother. Be sure of this." Bahá'u'lláh also directed that this be done. Accordingly, we left Ja'far in the hospital and went on to the 'Akká prison. Two months later, he and his brother Ḥájí Taqí arrived at the fortress, and joined the other prisoners. The safely delivered Ḥájí grew more loving, more ardent with every passing day. From dusk till dawn he would stay awake, chanting prayers, shedding his tears. Then one night he fell from the roof of the caravanserai and ascended to the Kingdom of miracles and signs.

Ḥájí Taqí, born under a fortunate star, was in every sense a true brother to Ḥájí Ja'far. He lived in the same spiritual condition, but he was calmer. After Ḥájí Ja'far's death, he would stay in one room, all alone. He was silence itself. He would sit there, all alone, properly and courteously, even during the night. One midnight he climbed up to the roof to chant prayers. The next morning they found him where he had fallen, on the ground by the wall. He was unconscious, and they could not tell whether this was an accident or whether he had thrown himself down. When he came to himself he said: "I was weary of this life, and I tried to die. Not for a moment do I wish to linger in this world. Pray that I may go on."

This, then, is the life story of those three brothers. All three were souls at rest; all three were well-pleased with their Lord and well-pleasing unto Him.[2] They were flames; they were captives of the Faith; they were pure and holy. And therefore, cut off from the world, turning their faces toward the Most High Kingdom, they ascended. May God wrap them in the garment of His grace in the realm of forgiveness, and immerse them in the waters of His mercy forever and ever. Greetings be unto them, and praise.

[2] Qur'án 89:27-30.

Ḥájí Mírzá Muḥammad-Taqí, the Afnán

AMONG THOSE souls that are righteous, that are luminous entities and Divine reflections, was Jináb-i-Muḥammad-Taqí, the Afnán.[1] His title was Vakílu'd-Dawlih. This eminent Bough was an offshoot of the Holy Tree; in him an excellent character was allied to a noble lineage. His kinship was a true kinship. He was among those souls who, after one reading of the Book of Íqán, became believers, bewitched by the sweet savors of God, rejoicing at the recital of His verses. His agitation was such that he cried out, "Lord, Lord, here am I!" Joyously, he left Persia and hurried away to 'Iráq. Because he was filled with longing love, he sped over the mountains and across the desert wastes, not pausing to rest until he came to Baghdád.

He entered the presence of Bahá'u'lláh, and achieved acceptance in His sight. What holy ecstasy he had, what fervor, what detachment from the world! It was beyond description. His blessed face was so comely, so luminous that the friends in 'Iráq gave him a name: they called him "the Afnán of all delights." He was truly a blessed soul, a man worthy to be revered. He never failed in his duty, from the beginning of life till his last breath. As his days

[1] The Afnán are the Báb's kindred.

began, he became enamored of the sweet savors of God, and as they closed, he rendered a supreme service to the Cause of God. His life was righteous, his speech agreeable, his deeds worthy. Never did he fail in servitude, in devotion, and he would set about a major undertaking with alacrity and joy. His life, his behavior, what he did, what he left undone, his dealings with others—were all a way of teaching the Faith, and served as an example, an admonishment to the rest.

After he had achieved the honor, in Baghdád, of meeting Bahá'u'lláh, he returned to Persia, where he proceeded to teach the Faith with an eloquent tongue. And this is how to teach: with an eloquent tongue, a ready pen, a goodly character, pleasing words, and righteous ways and deeds. Even enemies bore witness to his high-mindedness and his spiritual qualities, and they would way: "There is none to compare with this man for his words and acts, his righteousness, trustworthiness, and strong faith; in all things he is unique; what a pity that he is a Bahá'í!" That is: "What a pity that he is not as we are, perverse, uncaring, committing sins, engrossed in sensuality, the creatures of our passions!" Gracious God! They saw with their own eyes that the moment he learned of the Faith he was transformed, he was severed from the world, he began to emit rays from the Sun of Truth; and still, they failed to profit by the example he set.

During his days in Yazd he was, outwardly, engaged in commercial pursuits, but actually teaching the Faith. His only aim was to exalt the Word of God, his only wish, to spread the Divine sweet savors, his only thought, to come nearer and ever nearer to the mansions of the Lord. There was no remembrance on his lips but the verses of God. He was an embodiment of the good pleasure of Bahá'u'lláh; a dawning-point of the grace of the Greatest Name. Many and many a time, Bahá'u'lláh expressed to those about

Him, His extreme satisfaction with the Afnán; and consequently, everyone was certain that he would in future initiate some highly important task.

After the ascension of Bahá'u'lláh, the Afnán, loyal and staunch in the Covenant, rendered even more services than he had before; this in spite of many obstacles, and an overwhelming load of work, and an infinite variety of matters all claiming his attention. He gave up his comfort, his business, his properties, estates, lands, hastened away to 'Ishqábád and set about building the Mashriqu'l-Adhkár; this was a service of very great magnitude, for he thus became the first individual to erect a Bahá'í House of Worship, the first builder of a House to unify man. With the believers in 'Ishqábád assisting him, he succeeded in carrying off the palm. For a long period in 'Ishqábád, he had no rest. Day and night, he urged the believers on. Then they too exerted their efforts, and made sacrifices above and beyond their power; and God's edifice arose, and word of it spread throughout East and West. The Afnán expended everything he possessed to rear this building, except for a trifling sum. This is the way to make a sacrifice. This is what it means to be faithful.

Afterward he journeyed to the Holy Land, and there beside that place where the chosen angels circle, in the shelter of the Shrine of the Báb, he passed his days, holy and pure, supplicating and entreating the Lord. God's praise was always on his lips, and he chanted prayers with both his tongue and heart. He was wonderfully spiritual, strangely ashine. He is one of those souls who, before ever the drumbeat of "Am I not your Lord?" was sounded, drummed back: "Yea, verily Thou art!"[2] It was in the 'Iráq period, during the years between the seventies and the eighties of the Hijra, that he first caught fire and loved

[2] Qur'án 7:171.

the Light of the World, beheld the glory dawning in Bahá'u'lláh and witnessed the fulfillment of the words, "I am He that liveth in the Abhá Realm of Glory!"

The Afnán was an uncommonly happy man. Whenever I was saddened, I would meet with him, and on the instant, joy would return again. Praise be to God, at the last, close by the Shrine of the Báb, he hastened away in light to the Abhá Realm; but the loss of him deeply grieved 'Abdu'l-Bahá.

His bright grave is in Haifa, beside the Ḥaẓíratu'l-Quds, near Elijah's Cave. A tomb must be erected there, and built solidly and well. May God shed upon his resting-place rays from the Paradise of Splendors, and lave that holy dust with the rains that beat down from the retreats of the Exalted Companion. Upon him be the glory of the All-Glorious.

'Abdu'lláh Baghdádí

When he was very young, people thought of 'Abdu'lláh Baghdádí as a libertine, solely devoted to pleasure. He was regarded by all as the sport of inordinate desires, mired down in his physical passions. But the moment he became a believer, he was carried away by the sweet savors of God, and was changed into a new creation. He found himself in a strange rapture, completely transformed. He had been of the world, now he was of Heaven; he had lived by the flesh, now he lived by the spirit; he had walked in darkness; now he walked in light. He had been a slave to his senses, now he was a thrall of God. He had been clay and earthenware before, now he was a dear-bought pearl; a dull and lusterless stone before, now a ruby glowing.

Even among the non-believers, people were astonished at the change. What could have come over this youth, they wanted to know; how did it happen that he was suddenly detached from the world, eager and devoted? "He was tainted, corrupted," they said; "today he is abstemious and chaste. He was sunk in his appetites, but is now the soul of purity, living a righteous life. He has left the world behind him. He has broken up the feast, dismissed the revelers, and folded the banquet cloth away. His mind is distracted by love."

Briefly, he let go his pleasures and possessions, and journeyed to 'Akká on foot. His face had turned so bright, his nature so luminous, that it was a joy to look at him. I used to say: "Áqá 'Abdu'lláh, what condition are you in?" And he would answer to this effect: "I was in darkness; now, by the favor of the Blessed Beauty, I am in light. I was a heap of dust; He changed me to a fertile field. I was in constant torment; I am now at peace. I was in love with my chains; He has broken them. I was avid for this one and that; now I cling to the Lord. I was a bird in a cage; He let me out. Today, though I live in the desert, and I have the bare ground for my bed and pillow, it feels like silk. In the old time, my coverlet was satin, and my soul was on the rack. Now I am homeless, and happy."

But his burning heart broke when he saw how victimized was Bahá'u'lláh, how patiently He suffered. 'Abdu'lláh yearned to die for Him. And thus it came about that he offered up his life for his tender Companion, and hastened away, out of this dark world to the country of light. His luminous grave is in 'Akká. Upon him be the glory of the All-Glorious; upon him be mercy, out of the grace of the Lord.

Muḥammad-Muṣṭafá Baghdádí

Muḥammad-Muṣṭafá was a blazing light. He was the son of the famous scholar Shaykh Muḥammad-i-Shibl; he lived in 'Iráq, and from his earliest youth was clearly unique and beyond compare; wise, brave, deserving in every way, he was known far and wide. From childhood, guided by his father, he had lit the light of faith in the chapel of his heart. He had rid himself of the hindering veils of illusion, gazed about with perceptive eyes, witnessed great new signs of God and, regardless of the consequences, had cried aloud: "The earth hath shone out with the light of her Lord!" [1]

Gracious God! The opposition was powerful, the penalty obvious, the friends, every one of them, terrified, and off in some corner hiding their belief; at such a time this intrepid personality boldly went about his business, and like a man, faced up to every tyrant. The one individual who, in the year seventy, was famed in 'Iráq for his love

[1] Qur'án 39:69.

of Bahá'u'lláh, was this honored person. A few other souls, then in Baghdád and its environs, had crept away into nooks and crannies and, imprisoned in their own lethargy, there they remained. But this admirable Muḥammad-Muṣṭafá would boldly, proudly come and go like a man, and the hostile, because of his physical strength and his courage, were afraid to attack him.

After Bahá'u'lláh's return from His journey to Kurdistán, the virile strength and bearing of that gallant individual was still further enhanced. Whenever leave was granted, he would attend upon Bahá'u'lláh, and would hear from His lips expressions of favor and grace. He was the leader, among all the friends in 'Iráq, and after the great separation, when the convoy of the Beloved left for Constantinople, he remained loyal and staunch, and withstood the foe. He girded himself for service and openly, publicly, observed by all, taught the Faith.

As soon as Bahá'u'lláh's declaration that He was "He Whom God Shall Manifest" [2] had become known far and wide, Muḥammad-Muṣṭafá—being among those souls who had become believers prior to this Declaration, and before the call was raised—cried out: "Verily, we believe!" Because, even before this Declaration, the very light itself pierced through the veils that had closed off the peoples of the world, so that every seeing eye beheld the splendor, and every longing soul could look upon its Well-Beloved.

With all his strength, then, Muḥammad-Muṣṭafá arose to serve the Cause. He rested neither day nor night. After the Ancient Beauty had departed to the Most Great Prison; after the friends had been taken prisoner in Baghdád and sent away to Mosul; after the hostility of outstanding enemies and the opposition of the populace of

[2] The Promised One of the Báb.

Baghdád, he did not falter, but continued to stand his ground. A long time passed in this way. But with his yearning for Bahá'u'lláh, the tumult in his heart was such that he set out alone for the Most Great Prison. He reached there during the period of extreme restrictions, and had the honor of entering the presence of Bahá'u'lláh.

He asked then for leave to find a lodging somewhere in the neighborhood of 'Akká, and was permitted to reside in Beirut. There he went and faithfully served the Cause, assisting all the pilgrims as they arrived and departed. He was an excellent servitor, a generous and kindly host, and he sacrificed himself to see to their affairs as they passed through. For all this he became known everywhere.

When the Sun of Truth had set and the Light of the Concourse on high had ascended, Muḥammad-Muṣṭafá remained loyal to the Covenant. He stood so firm against the waverers that they dared not draw a breath. He was like a shooting star, a missile hurled against the demons; [3] against the violators, an avenging sword. Not one of the violators so much as dared pass through the street where he lived and if they chanced to meet him they were like those described in the Qur'án: "deaf, dumb, blind: therefore they shall not retrace their steps from error!" [4] He was the very embodiment of: "The blame of the blamer shall not deflect him from the path of God, and the terrible might of the reviler shall not shake him."

Living in the same manner as before, he served the believers with a free mind and pure intent. With all his heart, he assisted the travelers to the Holy Land, those who had come to circumambulate that place which is ringed around by the Company on high. Later he moved

[3] Islámic symbolism: Satan is the "stoned one"; with shooting stars for stones, the angels repel demons from Paradise. Qur'án 3:31, 15:17, 34; 37:7; 67:5.

[4] Qur'án 2:17.

from Beirut to Iskandarún, and there he spent some time, until, drawn as if by a magnet to the Lord, detached from all save Him, rejoicing in His glad tidings, holding fast to the cord that none can sever—he ascended on the wings of the spirit to his Exalted Companion.

May God lift him up to the highest Heaven, to the fellowship of glory.[5] May God bring him into the land of lights, the mysterious Kingdom, the assemblage of the splendors of the mighty, all powerful Lord. Upon him be the glory of the All-Glorious.

Sulaymán Khán-i-Tunukábání

SULAYMÁN KHÁN was the emigrant and settler who was given the title of Jamáli'd-Dín. He was born in Tunukábán, into an old family of that region. He was cradled in wealth, bred to ease, reared in the comfortable ways of luxury. From his early childhood he had high ambitions and noble aims, and he was honor and aspiration personified. At first he planned to outdistance all his fellows and achieve some lofty rank. For this reason he left his birthplace and went to the capital, Ṭihrán, where he hoped to become a leader, surpassing the rest of his generation.

[5] Qur'án 4:71.

In Ṭihrán, however, the fragrance of God was borne his way, and he listened to the summons of the Well-Beloved. He was saved from the perturbations of high rank; from all the din and clatter, the glory, the pomps and palaces, of this heap of dust, the world. He threw off his chains, and by God's grace, discovered peace. To him, the seat of honor was now no different from the place where people removed their slippers at the door, and high office was a thing soon gone and forgotten. He was cleansed from the stain of living, his heart was eased, for he had burst the shackles that held him to this present life.

Putting on the garments of a pilgrim, he set out to find his loving Friend, and came to the Most Great Prison. Here for a time he rested, under the protection of the Ancient Beauty; here he gained the honor of entering the presence of Bahá'u'lláh, and listened to momentous teachings from His holy lips. When he had breathed the scented air, when his eyes were illumined and his ears attuned to the words of the Lord, he was permitted to make a journey to India, and bidden to teach the true seekers after truth.

Resting his heart on God, in love with the sweet savors of God, on fire with the love of God, he left for India. There he wandered, and whenever he came to a city he raised the call of the Great Kingdom and delivered the good news that the Speaker of the Mount had come. He became one of God's farmers, scattering the holy seed of the Teachings. This sowing was fruitful. Through him a considerable number found their way into the Ark of Salvation. The light of Divine guidance was shed upon those souls, and their eyes were brightened with beholding the mighty signs of God. He became the focal point of every gathering, the honored guest. To this day, in India, the results of his auspicious presence are clear to see, and those whom he taught are now, in their turn, guiding others to the Faith.

Following his Indian journey, Sulaymán Khán came back to Bahá'u'lláh, but when he arrived, the ascension had taken place. Continuously, he shed his tears, and his heart was a thurible for sorrow. But he remained loyal to the Covenant, well rooted in Heaven.

Not long before His passing, Bahá'u'lláh had said: "Should someone go to Persia, and manage to convey it, this message must be delivered to Amínu's-Sulṭán:[1] 'You took steps to help the prisoners; you freely rendered them a befitting service; this service will not be forgotten. Rest assured that it will bring you honor and call down a blessing upon all your affairs. O Amínu's-Sulṭán! Every house that is raised up will one day fall to ruin, except the house of God; that will grow more massive and be better guarded day by day. Then serve the Court of God with all your might, that you may discover the way to a home in Heaven, and found an edifice that will endure forever.' " After the departure of Bahá'u'lláh, this message was conveyed to Amínu's-Sulṭán.

In Ádhirbáyján the Turkish clerics had brought down Áqá Siyyid Asadu'lláh, hunted him down in Ardabíl and plotted to shed his blood; but the Governor, by a ruse, managed to save him from being physically beaten and then murdered: he sent the victim to Tabríz in chains, and from there had him conducted to Ṭihrán. Amínu's-Sulṭán came to the prisoner's assistance and, in his own office, provided Asadu'lláh with a sanctuary. One day when the Prime Minister was ill, Náṣiri'd-Dín Sháh arrived to visit him. The Minister then explained the situation, and lavished praise upon his captive; so much so that

[1] The Prime Minister.

the Sháh, as he left, showed great kindness to Asadu'lláh, and spoke words of consolation. This, when at an earlier time, the captive would have been strung up at once to adorn some gallows-tree, and shot down with a gun.

After a time Amínu's-Sulṭán lost the Sovereign's favor. Hated, in disgrace, he was banished to the city of Qum. Thereupon this servant dispatched Sulaymán Khán to Persia, carrying a prayer and a missive written by me. The prayer besought God's aid and bounty and succor for the fallen Minister, so that he might, from that corner of oblivion, be recalled to favor. In the letter we clearly stated: "Prepare to return to Ṭihrán. Soon will God's help arrive; the light of grace will shine on you again; with full authority again, you will find yourself free, and Prime Minister. This is your reward for the efforts you exerted on behalf of a man who was oppressed." That letter and that prayer are today in the possession of the family of Amínu's-Sulṭán.

From Ṭihrán, Sulaymán Khán journeyed to Qum, and according to his instructions went to live in a cell in the shrine of the Immaculate.[2] The relatives of Amínu's-Sulṭán came to visit there; Sulaymán Khán inquired after the fallen Minister and expressed the wish to meet him. When the Minister learned of this, he sent for Sulaymán Khán. Placing all his trust in God, Sulaymán Khán hastened to the Minister's house and, meeting him in private, presented the letter from 'Abdu'l-Bahá. The Minister rose, and received the letter with extreme respect. Then addressing the Khán he said: "I had given up hope. If this longing is fulfilled, I will arise to serve; I will preserve and uphold the friends of God." Then he expressed his gratitude, indebtedness and joy, and added, "Praise be to God,

[2] Qum is the shrine city of Fáṭimih, "the Immaculate." Sister of the eighth Imám, Imám Riḍá, she was buried here in 816 A.D.

I hope again; I feel that by His aid, my dream will come true."

In brief, the Minister pledged himself to serve the friends, and Sulaymán Khán took his leave. The Minister then desired to give him a sum of money to defray the expenses of his journey, but Sulaymán Khán refused, and despite the Minister's insistence, would accept nothing. The Khán had not yet reached the Holy Land on his return journey when Amínu's-Sulṭán was recalled from exile and immediately summoned to the Premiership again. He assumed the position and functioned with full authority; and at first he did indeed support the believers, but toward the end, in the case of the Yazd martyrdoms, he was neglectful. He neither helped nor protected the sufferers in any way, nor would he listen to their repeated pleas, until all of them were put to death. Accordingly he too was dismissed, a ruined man; that flag which had flown so proudly was reversed, and that hoping heart despaired.

Sulaymán Khán lived on in the Holy Land, near the Shrine which the Exalted Assembly circle about. He kept company with the believers until the day of inescapable death, when he set out for the mansions of Him Who liveth, and dieth not. He turned his back on this heap of dust, the world, and hurried away to the country of light. He broke out of this cage of contingent being and soared into the endless, placeless Realm. May God enfold him in the waters of His mercy, cause His forgiveness to rain down upon him, and bestow on him the wonders of abounding grace. Salutations be unto him, and praise.

'Abdu'r-Raḥmán, the Coppersmith

THIS WAS a patient and long-enduring man, a native of Káshán. He was one of the very earliest believers. The down was not yet upon his cheek when he drank of the love of God, saw with his own eyes the heavenly table spread out before him, and received his faith and his portion of abounding grace.

In a little while he left his home and set out for the rose garden that was Baghdád, where he achieved the honor of entering the presence of Bahá'u'lláh. He spent some time in 'Iráq, and won a crown of endless favor: he would enter the presence of Bahá'u'lláh and many a time would accompany Him on foot to the Shrine of the Two Káẓims; this was his great delight.

'Abdu'r-Raḥmán was among the prisoners exiled to Mosul, and later he fairly dragged himself to the fortress at 'Akká. Here he lived, blessed by Bahá'u'lláh. He carried on a small business, trifling, but he was content with it, happy and at peace. Thus, walking the path of righteousness, he lived to be eighty years old, at which time, serenely patient, he soared away to the Threshold of God. May the Lord enfold him there with His bounty and compassion, and clothe him in the garment of forgiveness. His luminous grave is in 'Akká.

Muḥammad-Ibráhím-i-Tabrízí

This man, noble and high-minded, was the son of the respected 'Abdu'l-Faṭṭáḥ who was in the 'Akká prison. Learning that his father was a captive there, he came with all speed to the fortress so that he too might have a share of those dire afflictions. He was a man wise, understanding, in a tumult from drinking the wine of the love of God, but with a wonderful, basic serenity and calm.

He had inherited the nature of his father, and he exemplified the saying that the child is the secret essence of its sire. For this reason, over a long period, he found delight in the neighborhood of the Divine Presence, enjoying utter peace. Daytimes, he would carry on his trade, and at night he would come in all haste to the door of the house, to be with the friends. He was close to all those who were staunch and true; he was full of courage; he was grateful to God, abstemious and chaste, expectant of and relying on the bounty and grace of the Lord. He made his father's lamp to shine, brightened the household of 'Abdu'l-Faṭṭáḥ, and left descendants to remain behind him in this swiftly passing world.

He always did what he could to provide for the happiness of the believers; he always saw to their well-being. He was sagacious, grave, and steadfast. By God's grace, he stayed loyal to the end, and sound in faith. May God give him to drink from the cup of forgiveness; may he sip from the spring of God's bounty and good pleasure; may God raise him up to the heights of Divine bestowal. His sweet-scented tomb is in 'Akká.

Muḥammad-'Alíy-i-Ardikání

IN THE flower of tender youth, Muḥammad-'Alí, the illumined, heard the cry of God, and lost his heart to heavenly grace. He entered the service of the Afnán, offshoot of the Holy Tree, and lived happy and content. This was how he came to the city of 'Akká, and was for quite a time present at the Sacred Threshold, winning a crown of lasting glory. The eye of Bahá'u'lláh's grace and favor was upon him. He served with a loyal heart. He had a happy nature, a comely face; he was a man believing, seeking, tested and tried.

During the days of Bahá'u'lláh, Muḥammad-'Alí remained steadfast, and after the Supreme Affliction his heart did not fail him, for he had drunk the wine of the Covenant and his thoughts were fixed on the bounties of God. He moved to Haifa and lived, a firm believer, near the Ḥaẓíratu'l-Quds by the Holy Shrine on Mount Carmel till his final breath, when death came and the carpet of his earthly life was rolled up and put away.

This man was a true servant of the Threshold, a good friend to the believers. All were pleased with him, finding him an excellent companion, gentle and mild. May God succor him in His exalted Kingdom, and give him a home in the Abhá Realm, and send upon him abounding grace from the gardens of Heaven—the place of meeting, the place of the mystical contemplation of God. His amber-scented dust is in Haifa.

Ḥájí Áqáy-i-Tabrízí

Early in his youth this spiritual man, who came from Tabríz, had sensed the mystic knowledge and drunk the heady wine of God, and he remained staunch as ever in the Faith during his years of helpless age.

He lived for a time in Ádhirbáyján, enamored of the Lord. When he became widely known thereabouts as one bearing the name of God, the people ruined his life. His relatives and friends turned against him, finding a new excuse to hound him with every passing day. Finally he broke up his home, took his family and fled to Adrianople. He reached there during the close of the Adrianople period and was taken prisoner by the oppressors.

Along with us homeless wanderers, and under the protection of the Ancient Beauty, he came to the Most Great Prison and was a confidant and companion, sharing with us the calamities and tribulations, humble and long-enduring. Afterward, when the restrictions were somewhat relaxed, he engaged in trade, and through the bounty of Bahá'u'lláh was comfortable and at peace. But his body had become enfeebled from the earlier hardships, and all the suffering, and his faculties had deteriorated; so that ultimately he fell ill, beyond hope of a remedy; and not far from Bahá'u'lláh, and shadowed by His protection, he hastened away from this least of worlds to the high Heavens, from this dark place to the land of lights. May God immerse him in the waters of forgiveness; may He bring him into the gardens of Paradise, and there keep him safe forevermore. His pure dust rests in 'Akká.

Qulám-'Alíy-i-Najjár

This man, a carpenter and a master craftsman, came from Ká<u>sh</u>án. For faith and certitude, he was like a sword drawn from the scabbard. He was well known in his own city as a man righteous, true and worthy of trust. He was high-minded, abstemious and chaste. When he became a believer, his urgent longing to meet Bahá'u'lláh could not be stilled; full of joyous love, he went out of the Land of Káf (Ká<u>sh</u>án) and traveled to 'Iráq, where he beheld the splendor of the rising Sun.

He was a mild man, patient, quiet, mostly keeping to

himself. In Baghdád, he worked at his craft, was in touch with the friends, and sustained by the presence of Bahá'u'lláh. For some time he lived in utter happiness and peace. Then those who had been taken prisoner were sent away to Mosul, and he was among the victims and like them exposed to the wrath of the oppressors. He remained in captivity for quite a while and when freed came to 'Akká. Here too he was a friend to the prisoners and in the Fortress he continued to practice his skill. As usual he was inclined to solitude, apt to stay apart from friend and stranger alike, and much of the time lived by himself.

Then the supreme ordeal, the great desolation, came upon us. Qulám-'Alí took on the carpentry work of the Holy Tomb, exerting all his sure powers. To this day, the glass roof which is over the inner courtyard of the Shrine of Bahá'u'lláh remains as the product of his skill. He was a man crystal clear of heart. His face shone; his inner condition was constant; at no time was he changeable or unstable. He was staunch, loving, and true till his last breath.

After some years in this neighborhood, he rose upward to the neighborhood of the all-embracing mercy of God, and became a friend to those who dwell in the high Heavens. He had the honor of meeting Bahá'u'lláh in both worlds. This is the most precious bestowal, the costliest of all gifts. To him be salutations and praise. His bright grave is in 'Akká.

Jináb-i-Muníb, upon him be the Glory of the All-Glorious

His name was Mírzá Áqá and he was spirit itself. He came from Káshán. In the days of the Báb, he was drawn to the sweet savors of God; it was then he caught fire. He was a fine youth, handsome, full of charm and grace. He was a calligrapher second to none, a poet, and he had as well a remarkable singing voice. He was wise and perceptive; staunch in the Faith of God; a flame of God's love, severed from all but God.

During the years when Bahá'u'lláh resided in 'Iráq, Jináb-i-Muníb left Káshán and hastened to His presence. He went to live in a small and humble house, barely managed to subsist, and set about committing to writing the words of God. On his brow, the bestowals of the Manifestation were clear to see. In all this mortal world he had only one possession, his daughter; and even his daughter he had left behind in Persia, as he hurried away to 'Iráq.

At the time when, with all pomp and ceremony, Bahá'u'lláh and His retinue departed from Baghdád, Jináb-i-Muníb accompanied the party on foot. The young man had been known in Persia for his easy and agreeable life and his love of pleasure; also for being somewhat soft and delicate, and used to having his own way. It is obvious what a person of this type endured, going on foot from Baghdád to Constantinople. Still, he gladly measured out the desert miles, and he spent his days and nights chanting prayers, communing with God and calling upon Him.

He was a close companion of mine on that journey. There were nights when we would walk, one to either side of the howdah of Bahá'u'lláh, and the joy we had defies description. Some of those nights he would sing poems; among them he would chant the odes of Ḥáfiẓ, like the one that begins, *"Come, let us scatter these roses, let us pour out this wine,"* [1] and that other:

To our King though we bow the knee,
We are kings of the morning star.
No changeable colors have we—
Red lions, black dragons we are!

The Blessed Beauty, at the time of His departure from Constantinople, directed Jináb-i-Muníb to return to Persia and promulgate the Faith. Accordingly he went back, and over a considerable period he rendered outstanding services, especially in Ṭihrán. Then he came again, from Persia to Adrianople, and entered the presence of Bahá'u'lláh, enjoying the privilege of attending upon Him. At the time of the greatest catastrophe, that is, the exile to 'Akká, he was made a prisoner on this Pathway and traveled, by now feeble and ill, with the party of Bahá'u'lláh.

He had been stricken by a severe ailment and was pitifully weak. Still, he would not agree to remaining behind in Adrianople where he could receive treatment, because he wanted to sacrifice his life and fall at the feet of his Lord. We journeyed along till we reached the sea. He was now so feeble that it took three men to lift him and carry

[1] The remainder of the verse is: *"Let us split the roof of Heaven and draw a new design."*

him onto the ship. Once he was on board, his condition grew so much worse that the captain insisted we put him off the ship, but because of our repeated pleas he waited till we reached Smyrna. In Smyrna, the captain addressed Colonel 'Umar Bayk, the government agent who accompanied us, and told him: "If you don't put him ashore, I will do it by force, because the ship will not accept passengers in this condition."

We were compelled, then, to take Jináb-i-Muníb to the hospital at Smyrna. Weak as he was, unable to utter a word, he dragged himself to Bahá'u'lláh, lay down at His feet, and wept. On the countenance of Bahá'u'lláh as well, there was intense pain.

We carried Jináb-i-Muníb to the hospital, but the functionaries allowed us not more than one hour's time. We laid him down on the bed; we laid his fair head on the pillow; we held him and kissed him many times. Then they forced us away. It is clear how we felt. Whenever I think of that moment, the tears come; my heart is heavy and I summon up the remembrance of what he was. A great man; infinitely wise, he was, steadfast, modest and grave; and there was no one like him for faith and certitude. In him the inner and outer perfections, the spiritual and physical, were joined together. That is why he could receive endless bounty and grace.

His grave is in Smyrna, but it is off by itself, and deserted. Whenever this can be done, the friends must search for it, and that neglected dust must be changed into a much-frequented shrine,[2] so that pilgrims who visit there may breathe in the sweet scent of his last resting-place.

[2] Qur'án 52:4.

Mírzá Muṣṭafá Naráqí

AMONG THAT company of pure and goodly souls was Mírzá Muṣṭafá, a leading citizen of Naráq and one of the earliest believers. His face shone with the love of God. His mind was concerned with the anemones of mystic meanings, fair as meadows and beds of flowers.

It was in the days of the Báb that he first set his lips to the intoxicating cup of spiritual truth, and he had a strange tumult in his brain, a fierce yearning in his heart. In the path of God he threw down whatever he possessed; he gambled everything away, gave up his home, his kin, his physical well-being, his peace of mind. Like a fish on the sand, he struggled to reach the water of life. He came to ʻIráq, joined the friends of his soul, and entered the presence of Bahá'u'lláh. For some time he lived there, joyful and content, receiving endless bounty. Then he was sent back to Persia, where, to the utmost of his capacity, he served the Faith. He was a whole and accomplished man, staunch, firmly rooted as the hills; sound, and worthy of trust. To him, in all that turmoil and panic, the wild dogs howling were only buzzing flies; tests and trials rested his mind; when cast into the fire of afflictions that broke out, he proved to be shining gold.

On the day when the convoy of Bahá'u'lláh was leaving

Constantinople for Adrianople, Mírzá Muṣṭafá arrived from Persia. There was no opportunity for him to reach Bahá'u'lláh except once; and he was thereupon directed to return to Persia. At such a moment he had the honor of being received.

When Mírzá Muṣṭafá reached Ádhirbáyján, he began to spread the Faith. Day and night he remained in a state of prayer, and there in Tabríz he drank of a brimming cup. His fervor increased, his teaching raised a tumult. Then the eminent scholar, the renowned Shaykh Aḥmad-i-Khurásání, came to Ádhirbáyján and the two of them joined forces. The result was such overwhelming spiritual fire that they taught the Faith openly and publicly and the people of Tabríz rose up in wrath.

The farráshes hunted them down, and caught Mírzá Muṣṭáfá. But then the oppressors said, "Mírzá Muṣṭafá had two long locks of hair. This cannot be the right man." At once, Mírzá Muṣṭafá took off his hat and down fell the locks of hair. "Behold!" he told them. "I am the one." They arrested him then. They tortured him and Shaykh Aḥmad until finally, in Tabríz, those two great men drained the cup of death and, martyred, hastened away to the Supreme Horizon.

At the place where they were to be killed, Mírzá Muṣṭafá cried out: "Kill me first, kill me before Shaykh Aḥmad, that I may not see them shed his blood!"

Their greatness has been recorded for all time in the Writings of Bahá'u'lláh. They received many a Tablet from Him, and after their death He set down, with His exalted pen, the anguish they endured.

From youth till old age, this illustrious man, Mírzá Muṣṭafá, devoted his entire life to service on the pathway of God. Today he dwells in the all-glorious Realm, in the neighborhood of the ineffable mercy of God, and he rejoices with exceeding gladness, and he celebrates the praise of his Lord. Blessedness be his, and a goodly home.[1] To him be tidings of great joy, from the Lord of Lords. May God grant him an exalted station, in that high Company.

Zaynu'l-Muqarribín

THIS DISTINGUISHED man was one of the greatest of all the Báb's companions and all the loved ones of Bahá'u'lláh. When he lived under Islám, he was already famed for his purity and holiness of life. He was talented and highly accomplished in many directions. He was the leader and spiritual exemplar of the entire population of Najaf-Ábád, and the eminent of that area showed him unbounded respect. When he spoke out, his was the deciding opinion; when he passed judgment, it took effect; for he was known to all as the standard, and the authority of last resort.

He had no sooner learned of the Báb's Declaration than he cried out from the depths of his heart, "O our Lord! we have indeed heard the voice of one that called. He called us to the Faith—'Believe ye on your Lord'—and we have believed." [1] He rid himself of all impeding veils; his doubts dispelled, he began to extol and glorify the Beauty promised from of old. In his own home, and at Iṣfáhán, he be-

[1] Cf. Qur'án 13:28.
[1] Qur'án 3:190.

came notorious for declaring far and wide that the advent of the long-desired One had come to pass. By the hypocrites, he was mocked, cursed and tormented. As for the people, "the mass, as a snake in the grass," who had worshiped him before, now rose up to do him harm. Every day brought on a fresh cruelty, a new torment from his oppressors. He endured it all, and went on teaching with great eloquence. He remained staunch, unmoved, as their wrath increased. In his hands he held out a full cup of Divine glad tidings, offering to all who came that heady draught of the knowledge of God. He was utterly without fear, knew nothing of danger, and swiftly followed the holy path of the Lord.

After the attempt on the Sháh, however, there was no shelter anywhere; no evening, no morning, without intense affliction. And since his staying on in Najaf-Ábád at such a time was a great danger to the believers, he left there and traveled to 'Iráq. It was during the period when the Blessed Beauty was in Kurdistán, when He had gone into seclusion and was living in the cave on Sar-Galú, that Jináb-i-Zayn arrived in Baghdád. But his hopes were dashed, his heart grieved, for all was silence: there was no word of the Cause of God, no name nor fame of it; there were no gatherings, no call was being raised. Yaḥyá, terror stricken, had vanished into some dark hiding place. Torpid, flaccid, he had made himself invisible. Try as he might, Jináb-i-Zayn could find not one soul. He met on a single occasion with His Eminence Kalím. But it was a period when great caution was being exercised by the believers, and he went on to Karbilá. He spent some time there, and occupied himself with copying out the Writings, after which he returned home to Najaf-Ábád. Here the foul persecutions and attacks of his relentless enemies could hardly be endured.

But when the Trump had been sounded a second time,[2] he was restored to life. To the tidings of Bahá'u'lláh's advent his soul replied; to the drum beat, "Am I not your Lord?" his heart drummed back: "Yea, verily!"[3] Eloquently, he taught again, using both rational and historical proofs to establish that He Whom God Shall Manifest—the Promised One of the Báb—had indeed appeared. He was like refreshing waters to those who thirsted, and to seekers, a clear answer from the Concourse on high. In his writing and speaking, he was first among the righteous, in his elucidations and commentaries a mighty sign of God.

In Persia his life was in imminent peril; and since remaining at Najaf-Ábád would have stirred up the agitators and brought on riots, he hastened away to Adrianople, seeking sanctuary with God, and crying out as he went, "Lord, Lord, here am I!" Wearing the lover's pilgrim dress, he reached the Mecca of his longing. For some time he tarried there, in the presence of Bahá'u'lláh, after which he was commanded to leave, with Jináb-i-Mírzá Ja'far-i-Yazdí, and promulgate the Faith. He returned to Persia and began to teach most eloquently, so that the glad tidings of the Lord's advent resounded to the high heavens. In the company of Mírzá Ja'far he traveled everywhere, through cities flourishing and ruined, spreading the good news that the Blessed Beauty was now manifest.

Once again, he returned to 'Iráq, where he was the center of every gathering, and rejoiced his hearers. At all times, he gave wise counsel; at all times he was consumed with the love of God.

When the believers were taken prisoner in 'Iráq and banished to Mosul, Jináb-i-Zayn became their chief. He remained for some time in Mosul, a consolation to the

[2] Cf. Qur'án 39:68.
[3] Qur'án 7:171.

rest, working to solve their many problems. He would kindle love in people's hearts, and make them kind to one another. Later he asked for permission to attend upon Bahá'u'lláh; when this was granted he arrived at the Prison and had the honor of entering the presence of his Well-Beloved. He then busied himself with writing down the sacred verses, and encouraging the friends. He was love itself to the emigrants, and warmed the travelers' hearts. He never rested for a moment, and received new grace and bounty every day, meanwhile taking down the Bahá'í Scriptures with faultless care.

From his early years till his last breath, this eminent man never failed in service to the Manifestation. After the ascension he was consumed with such grieving, such constant tears and anguish, that as the days passed by, he wasted away. He remained faithful to the Covenant, and was a close companion to this servant of the Light of the World, but he longed to rise out of this life, and awaited his departure from day to day. At last, serene and happy, rejoicing in the tidings of the Kingdom, he soared away to that mysterious land. There he was loosed from every sorrow, and in the gathering-place of splendors he was immersed in light.

Unto him be salutations and praise from the luminous Realm, and the glory of the All-Glorious from the Concourse on high, and great joy in that Kingdom which endures forever. May God provide him with an exalted station in the Abhá Paradise.

'Aẓím-i-Tafríshí

THIS MAN of God came from the district of Tafrísh. He was detached from the world, fearless, independent of kindred and stranger alike. He was one of the earliest believers, and belonged to the company of the faithful. It was in Persia that he won the honor of belief, and began to assist the friends; he was a servant to every believer, a trusted helper to every traveler. With Músáy-i-Qumí, upon whom be the glory of God, he came to 'Iráq, received his portion of bounty from the Light of the World, and was honored with entering the presence of Bahá'u'lláh, attending upon Him and becoming the object of bestowals and grace.

After a time, 'Aẓím and Ḥájí Mírzá Músá went back to Persia, where he continued to render service to the friends, purely for God's sake. Without wage or stipend he served Mírzá Naṣru'lláh of Tafrísh for a number of years, his faith and certitude growing stronger with every passing day. Mírzá Naṣru'lláh then left Persia for Adrianople, and in his company came Jináb-i-'Aẓím, and entered the presence of Bahá'u'lláh. He kept on serving with love and loyalty, purely for the sake of God; and when the convoy departed for 'Akká, 'Aẓím received the distinction of accompanying Bahá'u'lláh, and he entered the Most Great Prison.

In the prison he was chosen to serve the Household; he became the water carrier both within doors and on the outside. He undertook many hard tasks in the barracks. He had no rest at all, day or night. 'Aẓím—"the great, the magnificent"—was magnificent as to character. He was patient, long-suffering, forbearing, shunning the stain of this earth. And since he was the family water carrier, he had the honor of coming into Bahá'u'lláh's presence every day.

He was a good companion to all the friends, a consolation to their hearts; he brought happiness to all of them, the present and the absent as well. Many and many a time, Bahá'u'lláh was heard to express His approval of this man. He always maintained the same inner condition; he was constant, never subject to change. He was always happy-looking. He did not know the meaning of fatigue. He was never despondent. When anyone asked a service of him, he performed it at once. He was staunch and firm in his faith, a tree that grew in the scented garden of God's tenderness.

After he had served at the Holy Threshold for many long years, he hastened away, tranquil, serene, rejoicing in the tidings of the Kingdom, out of this swiftly fading life to the world that does not die. The friends, all of them, mourned his passing, but the Blessed Beauty eased their hearts, for He lavished grace and praise on him who was gone.

Mercies be upon 'Aẓím from the Kingdom of Divine compassion; God's glory be upon him, at nightfall and the rising of the sun.

Mírzá Ja'far-i-Yazdí

This knight of the battlefield was one of the most learned of seekers after truth, well versed in many branches of knowledge. For a long time he was in the schools, specializing in the fundamentals of religion and religious jurisprudence, and making researches into philosophy and metaphysics, logic and history, the contemplative and the narrated sciences.[1] He began, however, to note that his fellows were arrogant and self-satisfied, and this repelled him. It was then that he heard the cry out of the Supreme Concourse, and without a moment's hesitation he raised up his voice and shouted, "Yea, verily!"; and he repeated the words, "O our Lord! We have heard the voice of one that called. He called us to the Faith—'Believe ye on your Lord'—and we have believed." [2]

When he saw the great tumult and the riots in Yazd, he left his homeland and went to Najaf, the noble city; here for safety's sake he mingled with the scholars of religion, becoming renowned among them for his own wide knowledge. Then, listening to the voice from Baghdád, he hastened there, and changed his mode of dress. That is, he put a layman's hat on his head, and went to work as a carpenter

[1] *Manqúl va ma'qúl:* "desumed" versus "excogitated" knowledge.
[2] Qur'án 3:190.

to earn his living. He traveled once to Ṭihrán, returned, and sheltered by the grace of Bahá'u'lláh was patient and content, rejoicing in his garb of poverty. In spite of his great learning he was humble, self-effacing, lowly. He kept silent at all times, and was a good companion to every sort of man.

On the journey from 'Iráq to Constantinople, Mírzá Ja'far was one of Bahá'u'lláh's retinue, and in seeing to the needs of the friends, he was a partner to this servant. When we would come to a stopping-place the believers, exhausted by the long hours of travel, would rest or sleep. Mírzá Ja'far and I would go here and there to the surrounding villages to find oats, straw and other provisions for the caravan.[3] Since there was a famine in that area, it sometimes happened that we would be roaming from village to village from after the noon hour until half the night was gone. As best we could, we would procure whatever was available, then return to the convoy.

Mírzá Ja'far was patient and long-suffering, a faithful attendant at the Holy Threshold. He was a servant to all the friends, working day and night. A quiet man, sparing of speech, in all things relying entirely upon God. He continued to serve in Adrianople until the banishment to 'Akká was brought about and he too was made a prisoner. He was grateful for this, continually offering thanks, and saying, "Praise be to God! I am in the fully-laden Ark!"[4]

The Prison was a garden of roses to him, and his narrow cell a wide and fragrant place. At the time when we were in the barracks he fell dangerously ill and was confined to

[3] Bahá'u'lláh was accompanied by members of His family and twenty-six disciples. The convoy included a mounted guard of ten soldiers with their officer, a train of fifty mules, and seven pairs of howdahs, each pair surmounted by four parasols. The journey to Constantinople lasted from May 3, 1863 to August 16. Cf. *God Passes By*, p. 156.

[4] Qur'án 26:119; 36:41.

his bed. He suffered many complications, until finally the doctor gave him up and would visit him no more. Then the sick man breathed his last. Mírzá Áqá Ján ran to Bahá'u'lláh, with word of the death. Not only had the patient ceased to breathe, but his body was already going limp. His family were gathered about him, mourning him, shedding bitter tears. The Blessed Beauty said, "Go; chant the prayer of Yá S͟háfí—O Thou, the Healer—and Mírzá Ja'far will come alive. Very rapidly, he will be as well as ever." I reached his bedside. His body was cold and all the signs of death were present. Slowly, he began to stir; soon he could move his limbs, and before an hour had passed he lifted his head, sat up, and proceeded to laugh and tell jokes.

He lived for a long time after that, occupied as ever with serving the friends. This giving service was a point of pride with him: to all, he was a servant. He was always modest and humble, calling God to mind, and to the highest degree full of hope and faith. Finally, while in the Most Great Prison, he abandoned this earthly life and winged his way to the life beyond.

Greetings and praise be unto him; upon him be the glory of the All-Glorious, and the favoring glances of the Lord. His luminous grave is in 'Akká.

THE FAITHFUL

Ḥusayn-Áqáy-i-Tabrízí

THIS MAN who was close to the Divine Threshold was the respected son of 'Alí-'Askar-i-Tabrízí. Full of yearning love, he came with his father from Tabríz to Adrianople, and by his own wish, went on with joy and hope to the Most Great Prison. From the day of his arrival at the fortress of 'Akká he took over the coffee service, and waited upon the friends. This accomplished man was so patient, so docile, that over a forty-year period, despite extreme difficulties (for day and night, friend and stranger alike thronged the doors), he attended upon each and every one who came, faithfully helping them all. During all that time Ḥusayn-Áqá never offended a soul, nor did anyone, where he was concerned, utter a single complaint. This was truly a miracle, and no one else could have established such a record of service. He was always smiling, attentive as to the tasks committed to his care, known as a man to trust. In the Cause of God he was staunch, proud and true; in times of calamity he was patient and long-suffering.

After the ascension of Bahá'u'lláh the fires of tests leaped up and a whirlwind of violation battered the edifice down. This believer, in spite of a close tie of kinship, remained loyal, showing such strength and firmness that he manifested the words: "In the Cause of God, the blame of the blamer shall he not fear." [1] Not for a moment did he hesitate, nor waver in his faith, but he stood firm as a mountain, proud as an impregnable citadel, and rooted deep.

The Covenant-breakers took his mother away to their own place, where her daughter lived. They did everything they could think of to unsettle her faith. To an extent beyond belief, they lavished favors upon her, and plied her with kindnesses, hiding the fact that they had broken the Covenant. Finally, however, that respected handmaid of Bahá'u'lláh detected the odor of violation, whereupon she instantly quit the Mansion of Bahjí and hurried back to 'Akká. "I am the handmaid of the Blessed Beauty," she said, "and loyal to His Covenant and Testament. Though my son-in-law were a prince of the realm, what would that profit me? I am not to be won over by kinship and displays of affection. I am not concerned with external tokens of friendliness from those who are the very embodiment of selfish desire. I stand by the Covenant, and I hold to the Testament." She would not consent to meet with the Covenant-breakers again; she freed herself completely from them, and turned her face to God.

As for Ḥusayn-Áqá, never did he separate himself from 'Abdu'l-Bahá. He had the utmost consideration for me and was my constant companion, and it followed that his passing was a formidable blow. Even now, whenever he comes to mind I grieve, and mourn his loss. But God be praised that this man of God, in the days of the Blessed Beauty, remained at all times in close proximity to His House, and was the object of His good pleasure. Time and again, Bahá'u'lláh was heard to comment that Ḥusayn-Áqá had been created to perform this service.

[1] Cf. Qur'án 5:59.

After forty years of serving, he forsook this swiftly passing world and soared away to the realms of God. Greetings and praise be unto him, and mercy from his bountiful Lord. May his grave be encircled with lights that stream from the exalted Companion. His resting-place is in 'Akká.

Hájí 'Alí-'Askar-i-Tabrízí

The distinguished 'Alí-'Askar was a merchant from Tabríz. He was much respected in Ádhirbáyján by all who knew him, and recognized for godliness and trustworthiness, for piety and strong faith. The people of Tabríz, one and all, acknowledged his excellence and praised his character and way of life, his qualities and talents. He was one of the earliest believers, and one of the most notable.

When the Trumpet first sounded, he fainted away, and at the second blast, he was awakened to new life.[1] He became a candle burning with the love of God, a goodly tree in the Abhá gardens. He led all his household, his other kindred and his friends to the Faith, and successfully rendered many services; but the tyranny of the wicked

[1] Qur'án 39:68-69: "And there shall be a blast on the trumpet, and all who are in the heavens and all who are in the earth shall swoon away, save those whom God shall vouchsafe to live. Then shall there be another blast on it, and lo! arising they shall gaze around them: and the earth shall shine with the light of her Lord . . ."

brought him to an agonizing pass, and he was beset by new afflictions every day. Still, he did not slacken and was not dispirited; on the contrary, his faith, his certitude and self-sacrifice increased. Finally he could endure his homeland no more. Accompanied by his family, he arrived in Adrianople, and here, in financial straits, but content, he spent his days, with dignity, patience, acquiescence, and offering thanks.

Then he took a little merchandise with him from Adrianople, and left for the city of Jum'ih-Bázár, to earn his livelihood. What he had with him was trifling, but still, it was carried off by thieves. When the Persian Consul learned of this he presented a document to the Government, naming an enormous sum as the value of the stolen goods. By chance the thieves were caught and proved to be in possession of considerable funds. It was decided to investigate the case. The Consul called in Ḥájí 'Alí-'Askar and told him: "These thieves are very rich. In my report to the Government, I wrote that the amount of the theft was great. Therefore you must attend the trial and testify conformably to what I wrote."

The Ḥájí," replied: "Your Honor, Khán, the stolen goods amounted to very little. How can I report something that is not true? When they question me, I will give the facts exactly as they are. I consider this my duty, and only this."

"Ḥájí," said the Consul, "We have a golden opportunity here; you and I can both profit by it. Don't let such a once-in-a-lifetime chance slip through your hands."

The Ḥájí answered: "Khán, how would I square it with God? Let me be. I shall tell the truth and nothing but the truth."

The Consul was beside himself. He began to threaten and belabor 'Alí-'Askar. "Do you want to make me out a liar?" he cried. "Do you want to make me a laughing-stock? I will jail you; I will have you banished; there is no torment I will spare you. This very instant I will hand you over to the police, and I will tell them that you are an enemy of the state, and that you are to be manacled and taken to the Persian frontier."

The Ḥájí only smiled. "Jináb-i-Khán," he said. "I have given up my life for the truth. I have nothing else. You are telling me to lie and bear false witness. Do with me as you please; I will not turn my back on what is right."

When the Consul saw that there was no way to make 'Alí-Askar testify to a falsehood, he said: "It is better, then, for you to leave this place, so that I can inform the Government that the owner of the merchandise is no longer available and has gone away. Otherwise I shall be disgraced."

The Ḥájí returned to Adrianople, and spoke not a word as to his stolen goods, but the matter became public knowledge and caused considerable surprise.

That fine and rare old man was taken captive in Adrianople along with the rest, and he accompanied the Blessed Beauty to the 'Akká fortress, this prison-house of sorrows. With all his family, he was jailed in the path of God for a period of years; and he was always offering thanks, because the prison was a palace to him, and captivity a reason to rejoice. In all those years he was never known to express himself except in thankfulness and praise. The greater the tyranny of the oppressors, the happier he was. Time and again Bahá'u'lláh was heard to speak of him with loving kindness, and He would say: "I am pleased with him." This man, who was spirit personified, remained constant, true, and joyful to the end. When some years had passed, he exchanged this world of dust for the Kingdom that is undefiled, and he left powerful influences behind.

As a rule, he was the close companion of 'Abdu'l-Bahá. One day, at the beginning of our time in the Prison, I hurried to the corner of the barracks where he lived—the cell that was his shabby nest. He was lying there, running a high fever, out of his head. On his right side lay his wife, shaking and trembling with chills. To his left was his daughter, Fáṭimih, burning up with typhus. Beyond them his son, Ḥusayn-Áqá, was down with scarlet fever; he had forgotten how to speak Persian, and he kept crying out in Turkish, "My insides are on fire!" At the father's feet lay the other daughter, deep in her sickness, and along the side of the wall was his brother, Ma<u>sh</u>hadí Faṭṭáḥ, raving and delirious. In this condition, 'Alí-'Askar's lips were moving: he was returning thanks to God, and expressing joy.

Praise be to God! He died in the Most Great Prison, still patient and thankful, still with dignity and firm in his faith. He rose up to the retreats of the compassionate Lord. Upon him be the glory of the All-Glorious; to him be salutations and praise: upon him be mercy and forgiveness forever and ever.

Áqá 'Alíy-i-Qazvíní

THIS EMINENT man had high ambitions and aims. He was to a supreme degree constant, loyal and firmly rooted in his faith, and he was among the earliest and greatest of the believers. At the very dawn of the new Day of Guidance he became enamored of the Báb and began to teach. From morning till dark he worked at his craft, and almost every night he entertained the friends at supper. Being host in this way to friends in the spirit, he guided many seekers to the Faith, attracting them with the melody of the love of God. He was amazingly constant, energetic, and persevering.

Then the perfume-laden air began to stir from over the gardens of the All-Glorious, and he caught fire from the newly kindled flame. His illusions and fancies were burned away and he arose to proclaim the Cause of Bahá'u'lláh. Every night there was a meeting, a gathering that rivaled the flowers in their beds. The verses were read, the prayers chanted, the good news of the greatest of Advents was shared. He spent most of his time in showing kindness to friend and stranger alike; he was a magnanimous being, with open hand and heart.

The day came when he set out for the Most Great Prison, and arrived with his family at the 'Akká fortress. He had been afflicted with many a hardship on his journey, but his longing to see Bahá'u'lláh was such that he found the calamities easy to endure; and so he measured off the miles, looking for a home in God's sheltering grace.

At first he had means; life was comfortable and pleasant. Later on, however, he was destitute and subjected to terrible ordeals. Most of the time his food was bread, nothing else; instead of tea, he drank from a running brook. Still, he remained happy and content. His great joy was to enter the presence of Bahá'u'lláh; reunion with his Beloved was bounty enough; his food was to look upon the beauty of the Manifestation; his wine, to be with Bahá'u'lláh. He was always smiling, always silent; but at the same time, his heart shouted, leapt and danced.

Often, he was in the company of 'Abdu'l-Bahá. He was an excellent friend and comrade, happy, delightful; favored by Bahá'u'lláh, respected by the friends, shunning the world, trusting in God. There was no fickleness in him, his inner condition was always the same: stable, constant, firmly rooted as the hills.

Whenever I call him to mind, and remember that patience and serenity, that loyalty, that contentment, involuntarily I find myself asking God to shed His bounties upon Áqá 'Alí. Misfortunes and calamities were forever descending on that estimable man. He was always ill, continually subjected to unnumbered physical afflictions. The reason was that when at home and serving the Faith in Qazvín, he was caught by the malevolent and they beat him so brutally over the head that the effects stayed with him till his dying hour. They abused and tormented him in many ways and thought it permissible to inflict every kind of cruelty upon him; yet his only crime was to have become a believer, and his only sin, to have loved God. As the poet has written, in lines that illustrate the plight of Áqá 'Alí:

By owls the royal falcon is beset.
They rend his wings, though he is free of sin.
"Why"—so they mock—"do you remember yet
That royal wrist, that palace you were in?"
He is a kingly bird: this crime he did commit.
Except for beauty, what was Joseph's sin?

Briefly, that great man spent his time in the 'Akká prison, praying, supplicating, turning his face toward God. Infinite bounty enfolded him; he was favored by Bahá'u'lláh, much of the time admitted to His presence and showered with endless grace. This was his joy and his delight, his great good fortune, his dearest wish.

Then the fixed hour was upon him, the daybreak of his hopes, and it came his turn to soar away, into the invisible realm. Sheltered under the protection of Bahá'u'lláh, he went swiftly forth to that mysterious land. To him be salutations and praise and mercy from the Lord of this world and the world to come. May God light up his resting-place with rays from the Companion on high.

Áqá Muḥammad-Báqir and Áqá Muḥammad-Ismá'íl, the Tailor

These were two brothers who, in the path of God, captives along with the rest, were shut in the 'Akká fortress. They were brothers of the late Pahlaván Riḍá. They left Persia and emigrated to Adrianople, hastening to the loving-kindness of Bahá'u'lláh; and under His protection, they came to 'Akká.

Pahlaván Riḍá—God's mercy and blessings and splendors be upon him; praise and salutations be unto him—was a man to outward seeming untutored, devoid of learning. He was a tradesman, and like the others who came in at the start, he cast everything away out of love for God, attaining in one leap the highest reaches of knowledge. He is of those from the earlier time. So eloquent did he suddenly become that the people of Ká<u>sh</u>án were astounded. For example this man, to all appearances unschooled, betook himself to Ḥájí Muḥammad-Karím <u>Kh</u>án in Ká<u>sh</u>án and propounded this question:

"Sir, are you the Fourth Pillar? I am a man who thirsts after spiritual truth and I yearn to know of the Fourth Pillar." [1]

Since a number of political and military leaders were present, the Ḥájí replied: "Perish the thought! I shun all those who consider me the Fourth Pillar. Never have I made such a claim. Whoever says I have, speaks falsehood; may God's curse be on him!"

A few days later Pahlaván Riḍá again sought out the Ḥájí and told him: "Sir, I have just finished your book, *Irs̲h̲ádu'l-'Avám* (Guidance unto the Ignorant); I have read it from cover to cover; in it you say that one is obligated to know the Fourth Pillar or Fourth Support; indeed, you account him a fellow knight of the Lord of the Age.[2] Therefore I long to recognize and know him. I am certain that you are informed of him. Show him to me, I beg of you."

The Ḥájí was wrathful. He said: "The Fourth Pillar is no figment. He is a being plainly visible to all. Like me, he has a turban on his head, he wears an 'abá, and carries a cane in his hand." Pahlaván Riḍá smiled at him. "Meaning no discourtesy," he said, "there is, then, a contradiction in Your Honor's teaching. First you say one thing, then you say another."

Furious, the Ḥájí replied: "I am busy now. Let us discuss this matter some other time. Today I must ask to be excused."

The point is that Riḍá, a man considered to be unlettered, was able, in an argument, to best such an erudite

[1] In S̲h̲ayk̲h̲í terminology, the Fourth Support or Fourth Pillar was the perfect man or channel of grace, always to be sought. Ḥájí Muḥammad-Karím K̲h̲án regarded himself as such. Cf. Bahá'u'lláh, *Kitáb-i-Íqán (The Book of Certitude)*, p. 184, and 'Abdu'l-Bahá, *A Traveller's Narrative*, p. 4.

[2] The promised Twelfth Imám.

"Fourth Pillar." In the phrase of 'Allámiy-i-Ḥillí, he downed him with the Fourth Support.[3]

Whenever that lionhearted champion of knowledge began to speak, his listeners marveled; and he remained, till his last breath, the protector and helper of all seekers after truth. Ultimately he became known far and wide as a Bahá'í, was turned into a vagrant, and ascended to the Abhá Kingdom.

As for his two brothers: through the grace of the Blessed Beauty, after they were taken captive by the tyrants, they were shut in the Most Great Prison, where they shared the lot of these homeless wanderers. Here, during the early days at 'Akká, with complete detachment, with ardent love, they hastened away to the all-glorious Realm. For our ruthless oppressors, as soon as we arrived, imprisoned all of us inside the fortress in the soldiers' barracks, and they closed up every issue, so that none could come and go. At that time the air of 'Akká was poisonous, and every stranger, immediately following his arrival, would be taken ill. Muḥammad-Báqir and Muḥammad-Ismá'íl came down with a violent ailment and there was neither doctor nor medicine to be had; and those two embodied lights died on the same night, wrapped in each other's arms. They rose up to the undying Kingdom, leaving the friends to mourn them forever. There was none there but wept that night.

When morning came we wished to carry their sanctified bodies away. The oppressors told us: "You are forbidden to go out of the fortress. You must hand over these two corpses to us. We will wash them, shroud them and bury them. But first you must pay for it." It happened that we had no money. There was a prayer carpet which had been

[3] 'Allámiy-i-Ḥillí, "the Very Erudite Doctor," title of the famed Shí'ih theologian, Jamálu'd-Dín Ḥasan ibn-i-Yúsuf ibn-i-'Alí of Hilla (1250-1325 A.D.).

placed under the feet of Bahá'u'lláh. He took up this carpet and said, "Sell it. Give the money to the guards." The prayer carpet was sold for 170 piasters [4] and that sum was handed over. But the two were never washed for their burial nor wrapped in their winding sheets; the guards only dug a hole in the ground and thrust them in, as they were, in the clothes they had on; so that even now, their two graves are one, and just as their souls are joined in the Abhá Realm, their bodies are together here, under the earth, each holding the other in his close embrace.

The Blessed Beauty showered His blessings on these two brothers. In life, they were encompassed by His grace and favor; in death, they were memorialized in His Tablets. Their grave is in 'Akká. Greetings be unto them, and praise. The glory of the All-Glorious be upon them, and God's mercy, and His benediction.

Abu'l-Qásim of Sulṭán-Ábád

ANOTHER among the prisoners was Abu'l-Qásim of Sulṭán-Ábád, the traveling companion of Áqá Faraj. These two were unassuming, loyal and staunch. Once their souls had come alive through the breathings of the Faithful Spirit they hastened out of Persia to Adrianople, for such

[4] The Turkish ghurúsh or piaster of the time was forty paras, the para one-ninth of a cent. These figures are approximate only.

was the unabating cruelty of the malevolent that they could no longer remain in their own home. On foot, free of every tie, they took to the plains and hills, seeking their way across trackless waters and desert sands. How many a night they could not sleep, staying in the open with no place to lay their heads; with nothing to eat or drink, no bed but the bare earth, no food but the desert grasses. Somehow they dragged themselves along and managed to reach Adrianople. It happened that they came during the last days in that city, and were taken prisoner with the rest, and in the company of Bahá'u'lláh they traveled to the Most Great Prison.

Abu'l-Qásim fell violently ill with typhus. He died about the same time as those two brothers, Muḥammad-Báqir and Muḥammad-Ismá'íl, and his pure remains were buried outside 'Akká. The Blessed Beauty expressed approval of him and the friends, all of them, wept over his afflictions and mourned him. Upon him be the glory of the All-Glorious.

Áqá Faraj

In all these straits, Áqá Faraj was the companion of Abu'l-Qásim. When, in Persian 'Iráq, he first heard the uproar caused by the Advent of the Most Great Light, he shook and trembled, clapped his hands, cried out in exultation and hastened off to 'Iráq. Overcome with delight, he entered the presence of his holy Lord. He was gathered into the loving fellowship, and blissfully received the honor of attending upon Bahá'u'lláh. Then he returned, bearing glad tidings to Sulṭán-Ábád.

Here the malevolent were lying in wait, and disturbances broke out, with the result that the sainted Mullá-Bás͟hí and some other believers who had none to defend them were struck down and put to death. Áqá Faraj and Abu'l-Qásim, who had gone into hiding, then hurried away to Adrianople, to fall, ultimately, with the others and with their Well-Beloved, into the 'Akká prison.

Áqá Faraj then won the honor of waiting upon the Ancient Beauty. He served the Holy Threshold at all times and was a comfort to the friends. During the days of Bahá'u'lláh he was His loyal servitor, and a close companion to the believers, and so it was after Bahá'u'lláh's departure: he remained true to the Covenant, and in the domain of servitude he stood like a towering palm; a noble, superior man, patient in dire adversity, content under all conditions.

Strong in faith, in devotion, he left this life and set his face toward the Kingdom of God, to become the object of endless grace. Upon him be God's mercy and good pleasure, in His Paradise. Greetings be unto him, and praise, in the meadows of Heaven.

The Consort of the King of Martyrs

Among the women who came out of their homeland was the sorrowing Fáṭimih[1] Begum, widow of the King of Martyrs. She was a holy leaf of the Tree of God. From her earliest youth she was beset with uncounted ordeals. First was the disaster which overtook her noble father in the environs of Badasht, when, after terrible suffering, he died in a desert caravanserai, died hard—helpless and far from home.

The child was left an orphan, and in distress, until, by God's grace, she became the wife of the King of Martyrs. But since he was known everywhere as a Bahá'í, was an impassioned lover of Bahá'u'lláh, a man distracted, carried away, and since Náṣiri'd-Dín Sháh thirsted for blood—the hostile lurked in their ambush, and every day they informed against him and slandered him afresh, started a new outcry and set new mischief afoot. For this reason his family was never sure of his safety for a single day, but lived from moment to moment in anguish, foreseeing and dreading the hour of his martyrdom. Here was the family, everywhere known as Bahá'ís; their enemies, stony-hearted tyrants; their government inflexibly, permanently against them; their reigning Sovereign rabid for blood.

[1] Accent the first syllable: FÁ-teh-meh.

It is obvious how life would be for such a household. Every day there was a new incident, more turmoil, another uproar, and they could not draw a breath in peace. Then, he was martyred. The Government proved brutal and savage to such a degree that the human race cried out and trembled. All his possessions were stripped away and plundered, and his family lacked even their daily bread.

Fáṭimih spent her nights in weeping; till dawn broke, her only companions were tears. Whenever she gazed on her children, she would sigh, wearing away like a candle in devouring grief. But then she would thank God, and she would say: "Praised be the Lord, these agonies, these broken fortunes are on Bahá'u'lláh's account, for His dear sake." She would call to mind the defenseless family of the martyred Ḥusayn, and what calamities they were privileged to bear in the pathway of God. And as she pondered those events, her heart would leap up, and she would cry, "Praise be to God! We too have become companions of the Prophet's Household." [2]

Because the family was in such straits, Bahá'u'lláh directed them to come to the Most Great Prison so that, sheltered in these precincts of abounding grace, they might be compensated for all that had passed. Here for a time she lived, joyful, thankful, and praising God. And although the son of the King of Martyrs, Mírzá 'Abdu'l-Ḥusayn, died in the prison, still his mother, Fáṭimih, accepted this, resigned herself to the will of God, did not so much as sigh or cry out, and did not go into mourning. Not a word did she utter to bespeak her grief.

This handmaid of God was infinitely patient, dignified and reserved, and at all times thankful. But then Bahá'u'lláh left the world, and this was the supreme affliction, the

[2] Gibbon writes of the Imám Ḥusayn's martyrdom and the fate of his Household, that "in a distant age and climate the tragic scene . . . will awaken the sympathy of the coldest reader."

ultimate anguish, and she could endure no more. The shock and alarm were such that like a fish taken from the water she writhed on the ground, trembled and shook as if her whole being quaked, until at last she took leave of her children and she died. She rose up into the shadowing mercy of God and was plunged in an ocean of light. Unto her be salutations and praise, compassion and glory. May God make sweet her resting-place with the outpourings of His heavenly mercy; in the shade of the Divine Lote-Tree [3] may He honor her dwelling.

Shams-i-Ḍuḥá

KHURSHÍD BEGUM, who was given the title of Shams-i-Ḍuḥá,[1] the Morning Sun, was mother-in-law to the King of Martyrs. This eloquent, ardent handmaid of God was the cousin on her father's side of the famous Muḥammad-Báqir of Iṣfáhán, widely celebrated as chief of the ʻulamás in that city. When still a child she lost both her parents, and was reared by her grandmother in the home of that

[3] The Sadratu'l-Muntahá, translated *inter alia* as the Sidrah Tree which marks the boundary, and the Lote-Tree of the extremity. Cf. Qur'án 53:14. It is said to stand at the loftiest point in Paradise, and to mark the place beyond which neither men nor angels can pass. In Bahá'í terminology it refers to the Manifestation of God.

[1] Pronounced Shams-seh-Zohá.

famed and learned mujtahid, and well trained in various branches of knowledge, in theology, sciences and the arts.

Once she was grown, she was married to Mírzá Hádíy-i-Nahrí; and since she and her husband were both strongly attracted to the mystical teachings of that great luminary, the excellent and distinguished Siyyid Káẓim-i-Ra<u>sh</u>tí,[2] they left for Karbilá, accompanied by Mírzá Hádí's brother, Mírzá Muḥammad-'Alíy-i-Nahrí.[3] Here they used to attend the Siyyid's classes, imbibing his knowledge, so that this handmaid became thoroughly informed on subjects relating to Divinity, on the Scriptures and on their inner meanings. The couple had two children, a girl and a boy. They called their son Siyyid 'Alí and their daughter Fáṭimih Begum, she being the one who, when she reached adolescence, was married to the King of Martyrs.

<u>Sh</u>ams-i-Ḍuḥá was there in Karbilá when the cry of the exalted Lord was raised in <u>Sh</u>íráz, and she shouted back, "Yea, verily!" As for her husband and his brother, they immediately set out for <u>Sh</u>íráz; for both of them, when visiting the Shrine of Imám Ḥusayn, had looked upon the beauty of the Primal Point, the Báb; both had been astonished at what they saw in that transplendent face, in those heavenly attributes and ways, and had agreed that One such as this must indeed be some very great being. Accordingly, the moment they learned of His Divine summons, they answered: "Yea, verily!" and they burst into flame with yearning love for God. Besides, they had been present every day in that holy place where the late Siyyid taught, and had clearly heard him say: "The Advent is nigh, the affair most subtle, most elusive. It behoves each one to search, to inquire, for it may be that the Promised

[2] A forerunner of the Báb, and co-founder of the <u>Sh</u>ay<u>kh</u>í School. See glossary.

[3] His daughter, at a later date, became the consort of 'Abdu'l-Bahá. Cf. *God Passes By,* p. 130, and *The Dawn-Breakers,* p. 461.

One is even now present among men, even now visible, while all about Him are heedless, unmindful, with bandaged eyes, even as the sacred traditions have foretold."

When the two brothers arrived in Persia they heard that the Báb had gone to Mecca on a pilgrimage. Siyyid Muḥammad-'Alí therefore left for Iṣfáhán and Mírzá Hádí returned to Karbilá. Meanwhile Shams-i-Ḍuḥá had become friends with the "Nightingale of Paradise," sister to Mullá Husayn, the Bábu'l-Báb.[4] Through that lady she had met Ṭáhirih, Qurratu'l-'Ayn,[5] and had begun to spend most of her time in close companionship with them both, occupied in teaching the Faith. Since this was in the early days of the Cause, the people were not yet afraid of it. From being with Ṭáhirih, Shams profited immeasurably, and was more on fire with the Faith than ever. She spent three years in close association with Ṭáhirih in Karbilá. Day and night, she was stirred like the sea by the gales of the All-Merciful, and she taught with an eloquent tongue.

As Ṭáhirih became celebrated throughout Karbilá, and the Cause of His Supreme Holiness, the Báb, spread all over Persia, the latter-day 'ulamás arose to deny, to heap scorn upon, and to destroy it. They issued a fatvá or judgment that called for a general massacre. Ṭáhirih was one of those designated by the evil 'ulamás of the city as an unbeliever, and they mistakenly thought her to be in the home of Shams-i-Ḍuḥá. They broke into Shams's house, hemmed her in, abused and vilified her, and inflicted grievous bodily harm. They dragged her out of the house and through the streets to the bázár; they beat her with clubs; they stoned her, they denounced her in foul language, repeatedly assaulting her. While this was going on,

[4] "Gate of the Gate," a title of Mullá Ḥusayn, the first to believe in the Báb. For an account of his sister, cf. *The Dawn-Breakers,* p. 383, note.

[5] "Solace of the Eyes."

Ḥájí Siyyid Mihdí, the father of her distinguished husband, reached the scene. "This woman is not Ṭáhirih!" he shouted at them. But he had no witness to prove it,[6] and the farrás͟hes, the police and the mob would not let up. Then, through the uproar, a voice screamed out: "They have arrested Qurratu'l-'Ayn!" At this, the people abandoned S͟hams-i-Ḍuḥá.

Guards were placed at the door of Ṭáhirih's house and no one was allowed to enter or leave, while the authorities waited for instructions from Bag͟hdád and Constantinople. As the interval of waiting lengthened out, Ṭáhirih asked for permission to leave for Bag͟hdád. "Let us go there ourselves," she told them. "We are resigned to everything. Whatever happens to us is the best that can happen, and the most pleasing." With government permission, Ṭáhirih, the Nightingale of Paradise, her mother and S͟hams-i-Ḍuḥá all left Karbilá and traveled to Bag͟hdád, but the snake-like mass of the populace followed them for some distance, stoning them from a little way off.

When they reached Bag͟hdád they went to live at the house of S͟hayk͟h Muḥammad-i-S͟hibl, the father of Muḥammad-Muṣṭafá; and since many crowded the doors there was an uproar throughout that quarter, so that Ṭáhirih transferred her residence elsewhere, to a lodging of her own, where she continually taught the Faith, and proclaimed the Word of God. Here the 'ulamás, s͟hayk͟hs and others would come to listen to her, asking their questions and receiving her replies, and she was soon remarkably well known throughout Bag͟hdád, expounding as she would the most recondite and subtle of theological themes.

When word of this reached the government authorities, they conveyed Ṭáhirih, S͟hams-i-Ḍuḥá and the Nightingale to the house of the Muftí, and here they remained

[6] Persian women of the day went heavily veiled in public.

three months until word as to their case was received from Constantinople. During Ṭáhirih's stay at the Muftí's, much of the time was spent in conversations with him, in producing convincing proofs as to the Teachings, analyzing and expounding questions relative to the Lord God, discoursing on the Resurrection Day, on the Balance and the Reckoning,[7] unraveling the complexities of inner truths.

One day the Muftí's father came in and belabored them violently and at length. This somewhat discomfited the Muftí and he began to apologize for his father. Then he said: "Your answer has arrived from Constantinople. The Sovereign has set you free, but on condition that you quit his realms." The next morning they left the Muftí's house and proceeded to the public baths. Meanwhile S͟hayk͟h Muḥammad-i-S͟hibl and S͟hayk͟h Sulṭán-i-'Arab made the necessary preparations for their journey, and when three days had passed, they left Bag͟hdád; that is, Ṭáhirih, S͟hams-i-Ḍuḥá, the Nightingale of Paradise, the mother of Mírzá Hádí, and a number of Siyyids from Yazd set out for Persia. Their travel expenses were all provided by S͟hayk͟h Muḥammad.

They arrived at Kirmáns͟háh, where the women took up residence in one house, the men in another. The work of teaching went on at all times, and as soon as the 'ulamás became aware of it they ordered that the party be expelled. At this the district head, with a crowd of people, broke into the house and carried off their belongings; then they seated the travelers in open howdahs and drove them from the city. When they came to a field, the muleteers set them down on the bare ground and left, taking animals and howdahs away, leaving them without food or luggage, and with no roof over their heads.

[7] Qur'án 7:7; 14:42; 21:48; 57:25, etc.

Ṭáhirih thereupon wrote a letter to the Governor of Kirmánsháh. "We were travelers," she wrote, "guests in your city. 'Honor thy guest,' the Prophet says, 'though he be an unbeliever.' Is it right that a guest should be thus scorned and despoiled?" The Governor ordered that the stolen goods be restored, and that all be returned to the owners. Accordingly the muleteers came back as well, seated the travelers in the howdahs again, and they went on to Hamadán. The ladies of Hamadán, even the princesses, came every day to meet with Ṭáhirih, who remained in that city two months.[8] There she dismissed some of her traveling companions, so that they could return to Baghdád; others, however, accompanied her to Qazvín.

As they journeyed, some horsemen, kinsfolk of Ṭáhirih's, that is, her brothers, approached. "We have come," they said, "at our father's command, to lead her away, alone." But Ṭáhirih refused, and accordingly the whole party remained together until they arrived in Qazvín. Here, Ṭáhirih went to her father's house and the friends, those who had ridden and those who had traveled on foot, put up at a caravanserai. Mírzá Hádí, the husband of Shams-i-Ḍuḥá, had gone to Máh-Kú, seeking out the Báb. On his return, he awaited the arrival of Shams in Qazvín, after which the couple left for Iṣfáhán, and when they reached there, Mírzá Hádí journeyed on to Badasht. In that hamlet and its vicinity he was attacked, tormented, even stoned, and was subjected to such ordeals that finally, in a ruined caravanserai, he died. His brother, Mírzá Muḥammad-'Alí, buried him there, along the roadside.

Shams-i-Ḍuḥá remained in Iṣfáhán. She spent her days and nights in the remembrance of God and in teaching His Cause to the women of that city. She was gifted with an eloquent tongue; her utterance was wonderful to hear.

[8] Cf. Nabíl, *The Dawn-Breakers,* chapter XV.

She was highly honored by the leading women of Iṣfáhán, celebrated for piety, for godliness, and the purity of her life. She was chastity embodied; all her hours were spent in reciting Holy Writ, or expounding the Texts, or unraveling the most complex of spiritual themes, or spreading abroad the sweet savors of God.

It was for these reasons that the King of Martyrs married her respected daughter and became her son-in-law. And when Shams went to live in his princely house, day and night the people thronged its doors, for the leading women of the city, whether friends or strangers, whether close to her or not, would come and go. For she was a fire lit by the love of God, and she proclaimed the Word of God with great ardor and verve, so that she became known among the non-believers as Fáṭimih, the Bahá'ís' Lady of Light.[9]

And so time passed, until the day when the "She-Serpent" and the "Wolf" conspired together and issued a decree, a fatvá, that sentenced the King of Martyrs to death. They plotted as well with the Governor of the city so that among them they could sack and plunder and carry off all that vast treasure he possessed. Then the Sháh joined forces with those two wild animals; and he commanded that the blood of both brothers, the King of Martyrs and the Beloved of Martyrs, be spilled out. Without warning, those ruthless men: the She-Serpent, the Wolf, and their brutal farráshes and constabulary—attacked; they chained the two brothers and led them off to prison, looted their richly furnished houses, wrested away all their possessions, and spared no one, not even infants at the breast. They tortured, cursed, reviled, mocked, beat the kin and others of the victims' household, and would not stay their hands.

[9] The reference is to Muḥammad's daughter, Fátimih, "the bright and fair of face, the Lady of Light."

In Paris, Ẓillu's-Sulṭán [10] related the following, swearing to the truth of it upon his oath: "Many and many a time I warned those two great scions of the Prophet's House, but all to no avail. At the last I summoned them one night, and with extreme urgency I told them in so many words: 'Gentlemen, the Sh̲áh has three times condemned you to death. His farmáns keep on coming. The decree is absolute and there is only one course open to you now: you must, in the presence of the 'ulamás, clear yourselves and curse your Faith.' Their answer was: 'Yá Bahá'u'l-Abhá! O Thou Glory of the All-Glorious! May our lives be offered up!' Finally I agreed to their not cursing their Faith. I told them all they had to say was, 'We are not Bahá'ís.' 'Just those few words,' I said, 'will be enough; then I can write out my report for the Sh̲áh, and you will be saved.' 'That is impossible,' they answered, 'because we *are* Bahá'ís. O Thou Glory of the All-Glorious, our hearts hunger for martyrdom! Yá Bahá'u'l-Abhá!' I was enraged, then, and I tried, by being harsh with them, to force them to renounce their Faith, but it was hopeless. The decree of the rapacious She-Serpent and Wolf, and the Sh̲áh's commands, were carried out."

After those two were martyred, Sh̲ams-i-Ḍuḥá was hunted down, and had to seek a refuge in her brother's house. Although he was not a believer, he was known in Iṣfáhán as an upright, pious and godly man, a man of learning, an ascetic who, hermit-like, kept to himself, and for these reasons he was highly regarded and trusted by all. She stayed there with him, but the Government did not abandon its search, finally discovered her whereabouts

[10] Eldest son of the Sh̲áh and ruler over more than two-fifths of the kingdom. He ratified the death sentence. Soon after these events, he fell into disgrace. Cf. *God Passes By,* p. 200; 232.

and summoned her to appear; the evil 'ulamás had a hand in this, joining forces with the civil authorities. Her brother was therefore obliged to accompany Shams-i-Ḍuḥá to the Governor's house. He remained without, while they sent his sister into the women's apartments; the Governor came there, to the door, and he kicked and trampled her so savagely that she fainted away. Then the Governor shouted to his wife: "Princess! Princess! Come here and take a look at the Bahá'ís' Lady of Light!"

The women lifted her up and put her in one of the rooms. Meanwhile her brother, dumbfounded, was waiting outside the mansion. Finally, trying to plead with him, he said to the Governor: "This sister of mine has been beaten so severely that she is at the point of death. What is the use of keeping her here? There is no hope for her now. With your permission I can get her back to my house. It would be better to have her die there, rather than here, for after all, she is a descendant of the Prophet, she is of Muḥammad's noble line, and she has done no wrong. There is nothing against her except her kinship to the son-in-law." The Governor answered: "She is one of the great leaders and heroines of the Bahá'ís. She will simply cause another uproar." The brother said: "I promise you that she will not utter a word. It is certain that within a few days she will not even be alive. Her body is frail, weak, almost lifeless, and she has suffered terrible harm."

Since the brother was greatly respected and trusted by high and low alike, the Governor released Shams-i-Ḍuḥá in his custody, letting her go. She lived for a while in his house, crying out, grieving, shedding her tears, mourning her dead. Neither was the brother at peace, nor would the hostile leave them alone; there was some new turmoil every day, and public clamor. The brother finally thought it best to take Shams away on a pilgrimage to Mashhad, hoping that the fire of civil disturbances would die down.

They went to Mashhad and settled in a vacant house near the Shrine of the Imám Riḍá.[11]

Because he was such a pious man the brother would leave every morning to visit the Shrine, and there he would stay, busy with his devotions until almost noon. In the afternoon as well, he would hasten away to the Holy Place, and pray until evening. The house being empty, Shams-i-Ḍuḥá managed to get in touch with various women believers and began to associate with them; and because the love of God burned so brightly in her heart she was unable to keep silent, so that during those hours when her brother was absent the place came alive. The Bahá'í women would flock there and absorb her lucid and eloquent speech.

In those days life in Mashhad was hard for the believers, with the malevolent always on the alert; if they so much as suspected an individual, they murdered him. There was no security of any kind, no peace. But Shams-i-Ḍuḥá could not help herself: in spite of all the terrible ordeals she had endured, she ignored the danger, and was capable of flinging herself into flames, or into the sea. Since her brother frequented no one, he knew nothing of what was going on. Day and night he would only leave the house for the Shrine, the Shrine for the house; he was a recluse, had no friends, and would not so much as speak to another person. Nevertheless there came a day when he saw that trouble had broken out in the city, and he knew it would end in serious harm. He was a man so calm and silent that he did not reproach his sister; he simply

[11] The eighth Imán, poisoned by order of the Caliph Ma'múm, A.H. 203, after the Imám had been officially designated as the Caliph's heir apparent. His shrine, with its golden dome, has been called the glory of the Shí'ih world. "A part of My body is to be buried in Khurásán," the Prophet traditionally said.

took her away from Mas͟hhad without warning, and they returned to Iṣfáhán. Here, he sent her to her daughter, the widow of the King of Martyrs, for he would no longer shelter her under his roof.

S͟hams-i-Ḍuḥá was thus back in Iṣfáhán, boldly teaching the Faith and spreading abroad the sweet savors of God. So vehement was the fiery love in her heart that it compelled her to speak out, whenever she found a listening ear. And when it was observed that once again the household of the King of Martyrs was about to be overtaken by calamities, and that they were enduring severe afflictions there in Iṣfáhán, Bahá'u'lláh desired them to come to the Most Great Prison. S͟hams-i-Ḍuḥá, with the widow of the King of Martyrs and the children, arrived in the Holy Land. Here they were joyously spending their days when the son of the King of Martyrs, Mírzá 'Abdu'l-Ḥusayn, as a result of the awful suffering he had been subjected to in Iṣfáhán, came down with tuberculosis and died in 'Akká.

S͟hams-i-Ḍuḥá was heavy of heart. She mourned his absence, she wasted away with longing for him, and it was all much harder because then the Supreme Affliction came upon us, the crowning anguish. The basis of her life was undermined; candle-like, she was consumed with grieving. She grew so feeble that she took to her bed, unable to move. Still, she did not rest, nor keep silent for a moment. She would tell of days long gone, of things that had come to pass in the Cause, or she would recite from Holy Writ, or she would supplicate, and chant her prayers—until, out of the Most Great Prison, she soared away to the world of God. She hastened away from this dust gulf of perdition to an unsullied country; packed her gear and journeyed to the land of lights. Unto her be salutations and praise, and most great mercy, sheltered in the compassion of her omnipotent Lord.

He is God!

Thou seest, O my Lord, the assemblage of Thy loved ones, the company of Thy friends, gathered by the precincts of Thine all-sufficing Shrine, and in the neighborhood of Thine exalted garden, on a day among the days of Thy Riḍván Feast—that blessed time when Thou didst dawn upon the world, shedding thereon the lights of Thy holiness, spreading abroad the bright rays of Thy oneness, and didst issue forth from Baghdád, with a majesty and might that encompassed all mankind; with a glory that made all to fall prostrate before Thee, all heads to bow, every neck to bend low, and the gaze of every man to be cast down. They are calling Thee to mind and making mention of Thee, their breasts gladdened with the lights of Thy bestowals, their souls restored by the evidences of Thy gifts, speaking Thy praise, turning their faces toward Thy Kingdom, humbly supplicating Thy lofty Realms.

They are gathered here to commemorate Thy bright and holy handmaid, a leaf of Thy green Tree of Heaven, a luminous reality, a spiritual essence, who ever implores Thy tender compassion. She was born into the arms of Divine wisdom, and she suckled at the breast of certitude; she flourished in the cradle of faith and rejoiced in the bosom of Thy love, O merciful, O compassionate Lord! And she grew to womanhood in a house from which the sweet savors of oneness were spread abroad. But while she was yet a girl, distress came upon her in Thy path, and misfortune assailed her, O Thou the Bestower, and in her defenseless youth she drank from the cups of sorrow and pain, out of love for Thy beauty, O Thou the Forgiver!

Thou knowest, O my God, the calamities she joyfully bore in Thy pathway, the trials she confronted in Thy love, with a face that radiated delight. How many a night, as others lay on their beds in soft repose, was she wakeful, humbly entreating Thy heavenly Realm. How many a day did Thy people spend, safe in the citadel of Thy sheltering care, while her heart was harried from what had come upon Thy holy ones.

O my Lord, her days and her years passed by, and whenever she saw the morning light she wept over the sorrows of Thy servants, and when the evening shadows fell she cried and called out and burned in a fiery anguish for what had befallen Thy bondsmen. And she arose with all her strength to serve Thee, to beseech the Heaven of Thy mercy, and in lowliness to entreat Thee and to rest her heart upon Thee. And she came forth veiled in holiness, her garments unspotted by the nature of Thy people, and she entered into wedlock with Thy servant on whom Thou didst confer Thy richest gifts, and in whom Thou didst reveal the ensigns of Thine endless mercy, and whose face, in Thine all-glorious Realm, Thou didst make to shine with everlasting light. She married him whom Thou didst lodge in the assemblage of reunion, one with the Company on high; him whom Thou didst cause to eat of all heavenly foods, him on whom Thou didst shower Thy blessings, on whom Thou didst bestow the title: Martyrs' King.

And she dwelt for some years under the protection of that manifest Light; and with all her soul she served at Thy Threshold, holy and luminous; preparing foods and a place of rest and couches for all Thy loved ones that came, and she had no other joy but this. Lowly and humble she was before each of Thy handmaids, deferring to each, serving each one with her heart and soul and her whole being, out of love for Thy beauty, and seeking to win Thy good pleasure. Until her house became known by Thy name, and the fame of her husband was noised abroad, as one belonging to Thee, and the Land of Ṣád (Iṣfáhán) shook and exulted for joy, because of continual blessings from this mighty champion of Thine; and the scented herbage of Thy knowledge and the roses of Thy bounty began to burgeon out, and a great multitude was led to the waters of Thy mercy.

Then the ignoble and and the ignorant amongst Thy creatures rose against him, and with tyranny and malice they pronounced his death; and void of justice, with harsh oppression, they shed his immaculate blood. Under the glittering sword that noble personage cried out to Thee: "Praised be Thou, O my God, that on the Promised Day, Thou hast helped me to attain this manifest grace; that Thou hast reddened the dust with my blood, spilled out upon Thy path, so that it puts forth crimson flowers. Favor and grace are Thine, to grant me this gift which in all the world I longed for most. Thanks be unto Thee that Thou didst succor me and confirm me and didst give me to drink of this cup that was tempered at the camphor fountain [1]—on the Day of Manifestation, at the hands of the cupbearer of martyrdom, in the assemblage of delights. Thou art verily the One full of grace, the Generous, the Bestower."

And after they had killed him they invaded his princely house. They attacked like preying wolves, like lions at the hunt, and they sacked and plundered and pillaged, seizing the rich furnishings, the ornaments and the jewels. She was in dire peril then, left with the fragments of her broken heart. This violent assault took place when the news of his martyrdom was spread abroad, and the children cried out as panic struck at their hearts; they wailed and shed tears, and sounds of mourning rose from out of that splendid home, but there was none to weep over

[1] Qur'án 76:5.

them, there was none to pity them. Rather was the night of tyranny made to deepen about them, and the fiery Hell of injustice blazed out hotter than before; nor was there any torment but the evil doers brought it to bear, nor any agony but they inflicted it. And this holy leaf remained, she and her brood, in the grip of their oppressors, facing the malice of the unmindful, with none to be their shield.

And the days passed by when tears were her only companions, and her comrades were cries; when she was mated to anguish, and had nothing but grief for a friend. And yet in these sufferings, O my Lord, she did not cease to love Thee; she did not fail Thee, O my Beloved, in these fiery ordeals. Though disasters followed one upon another, though tribulations compassed her about, she bore them all, she patiently endured them all, to her they were Thy gifts and favors, and in all her massive agony—O Thou, Lord of most beauteous names—Thy praise was on her lips.

Then she gave up her homeland, rest, refuge and shelter, and taking her young, like the birds she winged her way to this bright and holy Land—that here she might nest and sing Thy praise as the birds do, and busy herself in Thy love with all her powers, and serve Thee with all her being, all her soul and heart. She was lowly before every handmaid of Thine, humble before every leaf of the garden of Thy Cause, occupied with Thy remembrance, severed from all except Thyself.

And her cries were lifted up at dawntide, and the sweet accents of her chanting would be heard in the night season and at the bright noonday, until she returned unto Thee, and winged her way to Thy Kingdom; went seeking the shelter of Thy Threshold and soared upward to Thine everlasting sky. O my Lord, reward her with the contemplation of Thy beauty, feed her at the table of Thine eternity, give her a home in Thy neighborhood, sustain her in the gardens of Thy holiness as Thou willest and pleasest; bless Thou her lodging, keep her safe in the shade of Thy heavenly Tree; lead her, O Lord, into the pavilions of Thy godhood, make her to be one of Thy signs, one of Thy lights.

Verily Thou art the Generous, the Bestower, the Forgiver, the All-Merciful.

Ṭáhirih

A WOMAN chaste and holy, a sign and token of surpassing beauty, a burning brand of the love of God, a lamp of His bestowal, was Jináb-i-Ṭáhirih.[1] She was called Umm-Salmá; she was the daughter of Ḥájí Mullá Ṣáliḥ, a mujtahid of Qazvín, and her paternal uncle was Mullá Taqí, the Imám-Jum'ih or leader of prayers in the cathedral mosque of that city. They married her to Mullá Muḥammad, the son of Mullá Taqí, and she gave birth to three children, two sons and a daughter; all three were bereft of the grace that encompassed their mother, and all failed to recognize the truth of the Cause.

When she was still a child her father selected a teacher for her and she studied various branches of knowledge and the arts, achieving remarkable ability in literary pur-

[1] Pronounced TÁ-heh-reh.

suits. Such was the degree of her scholarship and attainments that her father would often express his regret, saying, "Would that she had been a boy, for he would have shed illumination upon my household, and would have succeeded me!" [2]

One day she was a guest in the home of Mullá Javád, a cousin on her mother's side, and there in her cousin's library she came upon some of the writings of Shaykh Aḥmad-i-Aḥsá'í.[3] Delighted with what he had to say, Ṭáhirih asked to borrow the writings and take them home. Mullá Javád violently objected, telling her: "Your father is an enemy of the Twin Luminous Lights, Shaykh Aḥmad and Siyyid Káẓim. If he should even dream that any words of those two great beings, any fragrance from the garden of those realities, had come your way, he would make an attempt against my life, and you too would become the target of his wrath." Ṭáhirih answered: "For a long time now, I have thirsted after this; I have yearned for these explanations, these inner truths. Give me whatever you have of these books. Never mind if it angers my father." Accordingly, Mullá Javád sent over the writings of the Shaykh and the Siyyid.

One night, Ṭáhirih sought out her father in his library, and began to speak of Shaykh Aḥmad's teachings. The very moment he learned that his daughter knew of the Shaykhí doctrines, Mullá Ṣáliḥ's denunciations rang out, and he cried: "Javád has made you a lost soul!" Ṭáhirih answered, "The late Shaykh was a true scholar of God, and I have learned an infinity of spiritual truths from reading his books. Furthermore, he bases whatever he says on the traditions of the Holy Imáms. You call yourself a

[2] Cf. *The Dawn-Breakers,* p. 81, note 2, and p. 285, note 2. Certain lines, there translated by Shoghi Effendi, are incorporated here.

[3] A forerunner of the Báb, and first of the two founders of the Shaykhí School. See glossary.

mystic knower and a man of God, you consider your respected uncle to be a scholar as well, and most pious—yet in neither of you do I find a trace of those qualities!"

For some time, she carried on heated discussions with her father, debating such questions as the Resurrection and the Day of Judgment, the Night-Ascent of Muḥammad to Heaven, the Promise and the Threat, and the Advent of the Promised One.[4] Lacking arguments, her father would resort to curses and abuse. Then one night, in support of her contention, Ṭáhirih quoted a holy tradition from the Imám Ja'far-i-Ṣádiq;[5] and since it confirmed what she was saying, her father burst out laughing, mocking the tradition. Ṭáhirih said, "Oh my father, these are the words of the Holy Imám. How can you mock and deny them?"

From that time on, she ceased to debate and contend with her father. Meanwhile she entered into secret correspondence with Siyyid Káẓim, regarding the solution of complex theological problems, and thus it came about that the Siyyid conferred on her the name "Solace of the Eyes" (Qurratu'l-'Ayn); as for the title Ṭáhirih ("The Pure One"), it was first associated with her in Badasht, and was subsequently approved by the Báb, and recorded in Tablets.

Ṭáhirih had caught fire. She set out for Karbilá, hoping to meet Siyyid Káẓim, but she arrived too late: ten days before she reached that city, he passed away. Not long before his death the Siyyid had shared with his disciples the good news that the promised Advent was at hand. "Go forth," he repeatedly told them, "and seek out your Lord." Thus the most distinguished of his followers gathered for retirement and prayer, for fasts and vigils, in the Masjid-i-Kúfih, while some awaited the Advent in Karbilá.

[4] Qur'án 17:1; 30:56; 50:19; etc.
[5] The sixth Imám.

Among these was Ṭáhirih, fasting by day, practicing religious disciplines, and spending the night in vigils, and chanting prayers. One night when it was getting along toward dawn she laid her head on her pillow, lost all awareness of this earthly life, and dreamed a dream; in her vision a youth, a Siyyid, wearing a black cloak and a green turban, appeared to her in the heavens; he was standing in the air, reciting verses and praying with his hands upraised. At once, she memorized one of those verses, and wrote it down in her notebook when she awoke. After the Báb had declared His mission, and His first book, "The Best of Stories,"[6] was circulated, Ṭáhirih was reading a section of the text one day, and she came upon that same verse, which she had noted down from the dream. Instantly offering thanks, she fell to her knees and bowed her forehead to the ground, convinced that the Báb's message was truth.

This good news reached her in Karbilá and she at once began to teach. She translated and expounded "The Best of Stories," also writing in Persian and Arabic, composing odes and lyrics, and humbly practicing her devotions, performing even those that were optional and supernumerary. When the evil 'ulamás in Karbilá got wind of all this, and learned that a woman was summoning the people to a new religion and had already influenced a considerable number, they went to the Governor and lodged a complaint. Their charges, to be brief, led to violent attacks on Ṭáhirih, and sufferings, which she accepted and for which she offered praise and thanks. When the authorities came hunting for her they first assaulted S͟hams-i-Ḍuḥá, mistaking her for Ṭáhirih. As soon, however, as they heard that Ṭáhirih had been arrested they let S͟hams go—for

[6] The "Aḥsanu'l-Qiṣaṣ," the Báb's commentary on the Súrih of Joseph, was called the Qur'án of the Bábís, and was translated from Arabic into Persian by Ṭáhirih. Cf. *God Passes By,* p. 23.

Ṭáhirih had sent a message to the Governor saying, "I am at your disposal. Do not harm any other."

The Governor set guards over her house and shut her away, writing Baghdád for instructions as to how he should proceed. For three months, she lived in a state of siege, completely isolated, with the guards surrounding her house. Since the local authorities had still received no reply from Baghdád, Ṭáhirih referred her case to the Governor, saying: "No word has come from either Baghdád or Constantinople. Accordingly, we will ourselves proceed to Baghdád and await the answer there." The Governor gave her leave to go, and she set out, accompanied by Shams-i-Ḍuḥá and the Nightingale of Paradise (the sister of Mullá Ḥusayn) and her mother. In Baghdád she stayed first in the house of Shaykh Muḥammad, the distinguished father of Áqá Muḥammad-Muṣṭafá. But so great was the press of people around her that she transferred her residence to another quarter, engaged night and day in spreading the Faith, and freely associated with the inhabitants of Baghdád. She thus became celebrated throughout the city and there was a great uproar.

Ṭáhirih also maintained a correspondence with the 'ulamás of Káẓimayn; she presented them with unanswerable proofs, and when one or another appeared before her she offered him convincing arguments. Finally she sent a message to the Shí'ih divines, saying to them: "If you are not satisfied with these conclusive proofs, I challenge you to a trial by ordeal."[7] Then there was a great outcry from the divines, and the Governor was obliged to send Ṭáhirih and her women companions to the house of Ibn-i-Álúsí, who was muftí of Baghdád. Here she remained about three months, waiting for word and directions from Constantinople. Ibn-i-Álúsí would engage her in learned dialogues,

[7] Qur'án 3:54: "Then will we invoke and lay the malison of God on those that lie!" The ordeal was by imprecation.

questions would be asked and answers given, and he would not deny what she had to say.

On a certain day the muftí related one of his dreams, and asked her to tell him what it meant. He said: "In my dream I saw the Shí'ih 'ulamás arriving at the holy tomb of Imám Ḥusayn, the Prince of Martyrs. They took away the barrier that encloses the tomb, and they broke open the resplendent grave, so that the immaculate body lay revealed to their gaze. They sought to take up the holy form, but I cast myself down on the corpse and I warded them off." Ṭáhirih answered: "This is the meaning of your dream: you are about to deliver me from the hands of the Shí'ih divines." "I too had interpreted it thus," said Ibn-i-Álúsí.

Since he had discovered that she was well versed in learned questions and in sacred commentaries and Texts, the two often carried on debates; she would speak on such themes as the Day of Resurrection, the Balance, and the Ṣirát,[8] and he would not turn away.

Then came a night when the father of Ibn-i-Álúsí called at the house of his son. He had a meeting with Ṭáhirih and abruptly, without asking a single question, began to curse, mock and revile her. Embarrassed at his father's behavior, Ibn-i-Álúsí apologized. Then he said: "The answer has come from Constantinople. The King has commanded that you be set free, but only on condition that you leave his realms. Go then, tomorrow, make your preparations for the journey, and hasten away from this land."

Accordingly Ṭáhirih, with her women companions, left the muftí's house, saw to arranging for their travel gear, and went out of Baghdád. When they left the city, a number of Arab believers, carrying arms, walked along beside their convoy. Among the escort were Shaykh Sulṭán,

[8] Qur'án 21:48; 19:37, etc. In Islám the Bridge to Ṣiráṭ, sharp as a sword and finer than a hair, stretches across Hell to Heaven.

Shaykh Muḥammad and his distinguished son Muḥammad-Muṣṭafá, and Shaykh Ṣáliḥ, and these were mounted. It was Shaykh Muḥammad who defrayed the expenses of the journey.

When they reached Kirmánsháh the women alighted at one house, the men at another, and the inhabitants arrived in a continuous stream to seek information as to the new Faith. Here as elsewhere the 'ulamás were soon in a state of frenzy and they commanded that the newcomers be expelled. As a result the kad-khudá or chief officer of that quarter, with a band of people, laid siege to the house where Ṭáhirih was, and sacked it. Then they placed Ṭáhirih and her companions in an uncovered howdah and carried them from the town to an open field, where they put the captives out. The drivers then took their animals and returned to the city. The victims were left on the bare ground, with no food, no shelter, and no means of traveling on.

Ṭáhirih at once wrote a letter to the prince of that territory, in which she told him: "O thou just Governor! We were guests in your city. Is this the way you treat your guests?" When her letter was brought to the Governor of Kirmánsháh he said: "I knew nothing of this injustice. This mischief was kindled by the divines." He immediately commanded the kad-khudá to return all the travelers' belongings. That official duly surrendered the stolen goods, the drivers with their animals came back out of the city, the travelers took their places and resumed the journey.

They arrived in Hamadán and here their stay was a happy one. The most illustrious ladies of that city, even the princesses, would come to visit, seeking the benefits of Ṭáhirih's teaching. In Hamadán she dismissed a part of her escort and sent them back to Baghdád, while she brought some of them, including Shams-i-Ḍuḥá and Shaykh-Ṣáliḥ, along with her to Qazvín.

As they traveled, some riders advanced to meet them, kinsmen of Ṭáhirih's from Qazvín, and they wished to lead her away alone, unescorted by the others, to her father's house. Ṭáhirih refused, saying: "These are in my company." In this way they entered Qazvín. Ṭáhirih proceeded to her father's house, while the Arabs who had formed her escort alighted at a caravanserai. Ṭáhirih soon left her father and went to live with her brother, and there the great ladies of the city would come to visit her; all this until the murder of Mullá Taqí,[9] when every Bábí in Qazvín was taken prisoner. Some were sent to Ṭihrán and then returned to Qazvín and martyred.

Mullá Taqí's murder came about in this way: One day, when that besotted tyrant had mounted his pulpit, he began to mock and revile the great Shaykh Aḥmad-i-Aḥsá'í. Shamelessly, grossly, screaming obscenities, he cried out: "That Shaykh is the one who has kindled this fire of evil, and subjected the whole world to this ordeal!" There was an inquirer in the audience, a native of Shíráz. He found the taunts, jeers and indecencies to be more than he could bear. Under cover of darkness he betook himself to the mosque, plunged a spearhead between the lips of Mullá Taqí and fled. The next morning they arrested the defenseless believers and thereupon subjected them to agonizing torture, though all were innocent and knew nothing of what had come to pass. There was never any question of investigating the case; the believers repeatedly declared their innocence but no one paid them any heed. When a few days had passed the killer gave himself up; he confessed to the authorities, informing them that he had committed the murder because Mullá Taqí had vilified Shaykh Aḥmad. "I deliver myself into your hands," he

[9] Cf. *The Dawn-Breakers,* p. 276. The murderer was not a Bábí, but a fervent admirer of the Shaykhí leaders, the Twin Luminous Lights.

told them, "so that you will set these innocent people free." They arrested him as well, put him in the stocks, chained him, and sent him in chains, along with the others, to Ṭihrán.

Once there he observed that despite his confession, the others were not released. By night, he made his escape from the prison and went to the house of Riḍá Khán—that rare and precious man, that star-sacrifice among the lovers of God—the son of Muḥammad Khán, Master of the Horse to Muḥammad Sháh. He stayed there for a time, after which he and Riḍá Khán secretly rode away to the Fort of Shaykh Ṭabarsí in Mázindarán.[10] Muḥammad Khán sent riders after them to track them down, but try as they might, no one could find them. Those two horsemen got to the Fort of Ṭabarsí, where both of them won a martyr's death. As for the other friends who were in the prison at Ṭihrán, some of these were returned to Qazvín and they too suffered martyrdom.

One day the administrator of finance, Mírzá Shafí', called in the murderer and addressed him, saying: "Jináb, do you belong to a dervish order, or do you follow the Law? If you are a follower of the Law, why did you deal that learned mujtahid a cruel, a fatal blow in the mouth? If you are a dervish and follow the Path, one of the rules of the Path is to harm no man. How, then, could you slaughter that zealous divine?" "Sir," he replied, "besides the Law, and besides the Path, we also have the Truth. It was in serving the Truth that I paid him for his deed." [11]

These things would take place before the reality of this Cause was revealed and all was made plain. For in those

[10] Cf. *The Dawn-Breakers,* p. 278.

[11] This refers to the doctrine that there are three ways to God: the Law (sharí'at), the Path (ṭaríqat), and the Truth (ḥaqíqat). That is, the law of the orthodox, the path of the dervish, and the truth. Cf. R. A. Nicholson, *Commentary on the Mathnaví of Rúmí,* s.v.

days no one knew that the Manifestation of the Báb would culminate in the Manifestation of the Blessed Beauty and that the law of retaliation would be done away with, and the foundation-principle of the Law of God would be this, that "It is better for you to be killed than to kill"; that discord and contention would cease, and the rule of war and butchery would fall away. In those days, that sort of thing would happen. But praised be God, with the advent of the Blessed Beauty such a splendor of harmony and peace shone forth, such a spirit of meekness and long-suffering, that when in Yazd men, women and children were made the targets of enemy fire or were put to the sword, when the leaders and the evil 'ulamás and their followers joined together and unitedly assaulted those defenseless victims and spilled out their blood—hacking at and rending apart the bodies of chaste women, with their daggers slashing the throats of children they had orphaned, then setting the torn and mangled limbs on fire—not one of the friends of God lifted a hand against them. Indeed, among those martyrs, those real companions of the ones who died, long gone, at Karbilá—was a man who, when he saw the drawn sword flashing over him, thrust sugar candy into his murderer's mouth and cried, "With a sweet taste on your lips, put me to death—for you bring me martyrdom, my dearest wish!"

Let us return to our theme. After the murder of her impious uncle, Mullá Taqí, in Qazvín, Ṭáhirih fell into dire straits. She was a prisoner and heavy of heart, grieving over the painful events that had come to pass. She was watched on every side, by attendants, guards, the farráshes, and her foes. While she languished thus, Bahá'u'lláh dispatched Hádíy-i-Qazvíní, husband of the celebrated Khátún-Ján, from the capital, and they managed, by a stratagem, to free her from that embroilment and got her to Ṭihrán in the night. She alighted at the mansion of Bahá'u'lláh and was lodged in an upper apartment.

When word of this spread throughout Ṭihrán, the Government hunted for her high and low; nevertheless, the friends kept arriving to see her, in a steady stream, and Ṭáhirih, seated behind a curtain, would converse with them. One day the great Siyyid Yaḥyá, surnamed Vaḥíd, was present there. As he sat without, Ṭáhirih listened to him from behind the veil. I was then a child, and was sitting on her lap. With eloquence and fervor, Vaḥíd was discoursing on the signs and verses that bore witness to the advent of the new Manifestation. She suddenly interrupted him and, raising her voice, vehemently declared: "O Yaḥyá! Let deeds, not words, testify to thy faith, if thou art a man of true learning. Cease idly repeating the traditions of the past, for the day of service, of steadfast action, is come. Now is the time to show forth the true signs of God, to rend asunder the veils of idle fancy, to promote the Word of God, and to sacrifice ourselves in His path. Let deeds, not words, be our adorning!"

The Blessed Beauty made elaborate arrangements for Ṭáhirih's journey to Badas͟ht and sent her off with an equipage and retinue. His own party left for that region some days afterward.

In Badas͟ht, there was a great open field. Through its center a stream flowed, and to its right, left, and rear there were three gardens, the envy of Paradise. One of those gardens was assigned to Quddús,[12] but this was kept a secret. Another was set apart for Ṭáhirih, and in a third was raised the pavilion of Bahá'u'lláh. On the field amidst the three gardens, the believers pitched their tents. Evenings,

[12] The eighteenth Letter of the Living, martyred with unspeakable cruelty in the market place at Bárfurús͟h, when he was twenty-seven. Bahá'u'lláh conferred on him a station second only to that of the Báb Himself. Cf. *The Dawn-Breakers,* pp. 408-415.

Bahá'u'lláh, Quddús and Ṭáhirih would come together. In those days the fact that the Báb was the Qá'im had not yet been proclaimed; it was the Blessed Beauty, with Quddús, Who arranged for the proclamation of a universal Advent and the abrogation and repudiation of the ancient laws.

Then one day, and there was a wisdom in it, Bahá'u'lláh fell ill; that is, the indisposition was to serve a vital purpose. On a sudden, in the sight of all, Quddús came out of his garden, and entered the pavilion of Bahá'u'lláh. But Ṭáhirih sent him a message, to say that their Host being ill, Quddús should visit her garden instead. His answer was: "This garden is preferable. Come, then, to this one." Ṭáhirih, with her face unveiled, stepped from her garden, advancing to the pavilion of Bahá'u'lláh; and as she came, she shouted aloud these words: "The Trumpet is sounding! The great Trump is blown! The universal Advent is now proclaimed!" [13] The believers gathered in that tent were panic struck, and each one asked himself, "How can the Law be abrogated? How is it that this woman stands here without her veil?"

"Read the Súrih of the Inevitable," [14] said Bahá'u'lláh; and the reader began: "When the Day that must come shall have come suddenly . . . Day that shall abase! Day that shall exalt! . . ." and thus was the new Dispensation announced and the great Resurrection made manifest. At the start, those who were present fled away, and some forsook their Faith, while some fell a prey to suspicion and doubt, and a number, after wavering, returned to the presence of Bahá'u'lláh. The Conference of Badas͟ht broke up, but the universal Advent had been proclaimed.

Afterward, Quddús hastened away to the Fort of Ṭa-

[13] Cf. Qur'án 74:8 and 6:73. Also Isaiah 27:13 and Zechariah 9:14.
[14] Qur'án, Súrih 56.

barsí[15] and the Blessed Beauty, with provisions and equipment, journeyed to Níyálá, having the intention of going on from there by night, making His way through the enemy encampment and entering the Fort. But Mírzá Taqí, the Governor of Ámul, got word of this, and with seven hundred riflemen arrived in Níyálá. Surrounding the village by night, he sent Bahá'u'lláh with eleven riders back to Ámul, and those calamities and tribulations, told of before, came to pass.

As for Ṭáhirih, after the breakup at Badasht she was captured, and the oppressors sent her back under guard to Ṭihrán. There she was imprisoned in the house of Maḥmúd Khán, the Kalántar. But she was aflame, enamored, restless, and could not be still. The ladies of Ṭihrán, on one pretext or another, crowded to see and listen to her. It happened that there was a celebration at the Mayor's house for the marriage of his son; a nuptial banquet was prepared, and the house adorned. The flower of Ṭihrán's ladies were invited, the princesses, the wives of vazírs and other great. A splendid wedding it was, with instrumental music and vocal melodies—by day and night the lute, the bells and songs. Then Ṭáhirih began to speak; and so bewitched were the great ladies that they forsook the cithern and the drum and all the pleasures of the wedding feast, to crowd about Ṭáhirih and listen to the sweet words of her mouth.

Thus she remained, a helpless captive. Then came the

[15] A systematic campaign against the new Faith had been launched in Persia by the civil and ecclesiastical authorities combined. The believers, cut down wherever they were isolated, banded together when they could, for protection against the Government, the clergy, and the people. Betrayed and surrounded as they passed through the forest of Mázindarán, some 300 believers, mostly students and recluses, built the Fort of Shaykh Ṭabarsí and held out against the armies of Persia for eleven months. Cf. *The Dawn-Breakers,* chapters XIX and XX; *God Passes By,* p. 37 et seq.

attempt on the life of the Sháh;[16] a farmán was issued; she was sentenced to death. Saying she was summoned to the Prime Minister's, they arrived to lead her away from the Kalántar's house. She bathed her face and hands, arrayed herself in a costly dress, and scented with attar of roses she came out of the house.

They brought her into a garden, where the headsmen waited; but these wavered and then refused to end her life. A slave was found, far gone in drunkenness; besotted, vicious, black of heart. And he strangled Ṭáhirih. He forced a scarf between her lips and rammed it down her throat. Then they lifted up her unsullied body and flung it in a well, there in the garden, and over it threw down earth and stones. But Ṭáhirih rejoiced; she had heard with a light heart the tidings of her martyrdom; she set her eyes on the supernal Kingdom and offered up her life.

Salutations be unto her, and praise. Holy be her dust, as the tiers of light come down on it from Heaven.

[16] On August 15, 1852, a half-crazed Bábí youth wounded the Sháh with shot from a pistol. The assailant was instantly killed, and the authorities carried out a wholesale massacre of the believers, its climax described by Renan as "a day perhaps unparalleled in the history of the world." Cf. Lord Curzon, *Persia and the Persian Question,* pp. 501-2, and *God Passes By,* p. 62 et seq.

GUIDE TO PERSIAN PRONUNCIATION

a	as in hat
á	rhymes with mom; or awe
ar	as in Harry
aw	rhymes with no
ch	as in church
ḍ	like z in zebra
dh	like z in zebra
gh	sounds like a French r
h	as in hat
ḥ	as in hat
	N.B. Always pronounce the h. Example: Teh-ron (Ṭihrán)
i	rhymes with bet
í	rhymes with meet
kh	sounds like ch in Scotch loch
Q	sounds like a French r
s	like s in yes
ṣ	like s in yes
t	as in tea
ṭ	as in tea
th	like s in yes
u	as "o" in short
ú	sounds like moot
	N.B. Equal emphasis on each syllable: Ṭá-heh-reh
	Apostrophe denotes a pause: Bahá' . . . í

The Arabic-Persian alphabet not only represents sounds for which there is no western equivalent, but contains four different z's, three s's, etc. This means that arbitrary marks, letters, and combinations of letters must be used to transliterate Arabic and Persian words into Western tongues. Pronunciation varies all over the Middle East, and heretofore western spelling has gone according to the nationality of the orientalist, the Englishman writing shah, the Frenchman, chah, the German schah, each nation contributing its own accent as well. To bring order out of chaos, the above system was devised by orientalists, and adopted by the Guardian for Bahá'í use. With it a uniform western spelling is achieved, and a student can tell at a glance how the word is written in the original. Letters not shown are pronounced as in English.

GLOSSARY

'Abá: cloak, mantle

Abhá: superlative of Bahá; Most Glorious; All-Glorious

Abjad reckoning: numerical value of letters in the Arabic-Persian alphabet

Afnán: the Báb's kindred. Cf. *God Passes By*, 239; 328

The Ancient Beauty: a title of Bahá'u'lláh

The Blessed Beauty: a title of Bahá'u'lláh

Dawlih: state; government

Farmán: order; command; royal decree

Farrásh: attendant; footman

Farsakh: same as parsang; a unit of measurement, varying from three to four miles, according to the terrain

Fatvá: judgment pronounced by a muftí

Ḥájí: title of a Muslim who has made the pilgrimage to Mecca

Ḥaẓíratu'l-Quds: the Sacred Fold; Bahá'í administrative center

Imám: title of the twelve Shí'ih successors of Muḥammad. Unlike the Caliph of the Sunní Muslims, an elected, outward and visible head—the vicegerency of the Prophet is to Shí'ihs a purely spiritual matter, conferred by Muḥammad and each of His successors until the twelfth. The Imám is the "divinely ordained successor of the Prophet, one endowed with all perfections and spiritual gifts, one whom all the faithful must obey, whose decision is absolute and final, whose wisdom is superhuman, and whose words are authoritative."

Imám: prayer-leader

Imám-Jum'ih: prayer-leader in the Friday or cathedral mosque

Jináb: courtesy title, varying in emphasis; somewhat equivalent to Your Honor, His Honor

Kad-Khudá: borough head; village head

Kalántar: mayor

Lote-Tree: refers to the Manifestation of God

Mashriqu'l-Adhkár: dawning-place of the praise of God; Bahá'í House of Worship

Muftí: expounder of Muslim law

Mujtahid: doctor of the law; cleric whose rank entitles him to practice religious jurisprudence. Most Persian mujtahids have received their diplomas from the leading jurists of Karbilá and Najaf

Mullá: Muslim priest

Nabíl: learned; noble. The Báb and Bahá'u'lláh sometimes referred to a person by a title whose letters, in the abjad reckoning, had the same numerical value as the individual's name. E.g., the numerical value of the letters in Muḥammad is 92, and that of the letters in Nabíl is also 92.

Qá'im: He Who Ariseth: a title of the Báb

Shaykhí School: a sect of Shí'ih Islám. The Shí'ihs were divided into two main branches, the "Sect of the Seven" and the "Sect of the Twelve." Sprung from the latter branch, the Shaykhí School was founded by Shaykh Aḥmad and Siyyid Káẓim, forerunners of the Báb. The Guardian writes in *God Passes By,* his history of the first hundred years of the Bábí-Bahá'í Faith, p. xii: "I shall seek to represent and correlate . . . those momentous happenings which have insensibly, relentlessly, and under the very eyes of successive generations, perverse, indifferent or hostile, transformed a heterodox and seemingly negligible offshoot of the Shaykhí school . . . into a world religion . . ."

Ṣiráṭ: bridge or path; denotes the religion of God

Siyyid: title of the Prophet Muḥammad's descendants

'Ulamá: divines, scholars

The text of *Memorials of the Faithful* has been set in eleven on thirteen point Fairfield, with chapter heads in Deepdene italic and initial letters in Weiss, printed on sixty pound Glatfelter antique book paper. Composition, printing and binding are by Kingsport Press, Kingsport, Tenn. It is bound in Interlaken natural buckram with Multicolor endleaf paper.

Calligraphic signature on half-title is by the well-known Bahá'í calligraphist, Mis͟hkín Qalam whose life is extolled in this book. It is an artistic arrangement of the phrase "Bismi'lláhi'l-Bahíyyi'l-Abhá" which means "In the name of God, the Glorious, the Most Glorious."